M4 SHERMAN
vs
TYPE 97 CHI-HA
The Pacific 1945

STEVEN J. ZALOGA

First published in Great Britain in 2012 by Osprey Publishing,
Midland House, West Way, Botley, Oxford, OX2 0PH, UK
44-02 23rd Street, Suite 219, Long Island City, NY 11101, USA

E-mail: info@ospreypublishing.com

OSPREY PUBLISHING IS PART OF THE OSPREY GROUP

A CIP catalog record for this book is available from the British Library

Print ISBN: 978 1 84908 638 7
PDF ebook ISBN: 978 1 84908 639 4
ePub ebook ISBN: 978 1 78096 422 5

Page layout by Ken Vail Graphic Design, Cambridge, UK
Index by Alan Thatcher
Typeset in ITC Conduit and Adobe Garamond
Maps by bounford.com
Originated by PDQ Media, Bungay, UK
Printed in China through Bookbuilders

12 13 14 15 16   10 9 8 7 6 5 4 3 2 1

Osprey Publishing is supporting the Woodland Trust, the UK's leading woodland
conservation charity, by funding the dedication of trees.

www.ospreypublishing.com

Author's note

The author would like to thank Tom Laemlein of Armor Plate
Press for use of several original photos from his collection.
Thanks also to Akira "Taki" Takizawa for help on several subjects.
Taki's internet site on Japanese tanks (www3.plala.or.jp/takihome)
is most informative for readers interested in Japanese World War II
tank history.

US Army units are identified by the traditional contractions, so
161st Infantry refers to the 161st Infantry Regiment; 2/161st
Infantry refers to the 2nd Battalion, 161st Infantry Regiment, and
B/161st Infantry refers to Company B, 1st Battalion, 161st
Infantry Regiment. Japanese names are rendered in Western
fashion, personal name followed by family name, rather than the
Japanese style of family name followed by personal name.

Editor's note

For ease of comparison please refer to the following conversion
table:

1 mile = 1.6km
1yd = 0.9m
1ft = 0.3m
1in. = 2.54cm/25.4mm
1 gallon (US) = 3.8 liters
1 ton (US) = 0.9 metric tons
1lb = 0.45kg

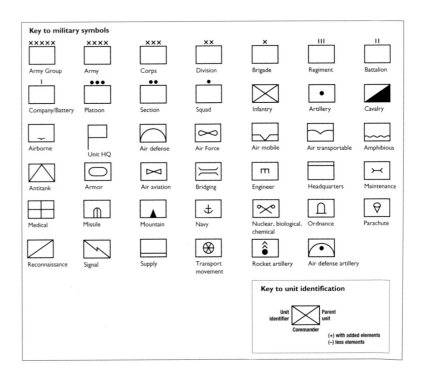

CONTENTS

INTRODUCTION

Most titles in the Duel series deal with weapons of similar combat effectiveness. But what happens when the weapons of one side are dramatically inferior to those of the other? Could the technological imbalance be overcome by innovative tactics? This title examines such a contest, the US Army's M4A3 Sherman medium tank against the Japanese Type 97-kai Shinhoto Chi-Ha in the Philippines in 1945.

Tank combat in the Pacific War of 1941–45 is not widely discussed. There has long been a presumption that the terrain conditions in many areas, especially the mountainous tropical jungles of the Southwest Pacific and Burma, were not well suited to tank use. Yet the terrain of the Pacific battlefields varied enormously, from the fetid jungles of New Guinea to the rocky coral atolls of the Central Pacific. In many of the critical campaigns of 1944–45, the terrain was suitable for tank use and they became a critical ingredient in the outcome of the fighting.

This book examines the largest single armored clash of the Pacific War – on Luzon in the Philippines in January–February 1945. This was the only time that the Imperial Japanese Army (IJA) committed an entire armored division against American or British forces. On the American side, the US Army eventually deployed 20 tank and tank-destroyer battalions to the Philippines fighting, roughly the equivalent of five armored divisions' worth of tanks. The Philippines campaign was characterized by a very broad range of terrain, from the flat rice paddies of Manila's central plains, to the tropical forests in the mountains of northern Luzon, to the fortified walls and urban congestion of Manila, and it therefore required numerous different tank tactics. The focus of the Duel is the clash between the Japanese 7th Tank Regiment and the US Army's 716th Tank Battalion at San Manuel on Luzon in late January 1945.

The IJA made extensive use of tanks in China through the 1930s. Due to China's poor road network and completely inadequate arsenal of antitank weapons, Japanese tanks were very lightly armed and armored. Clashes with the Red Army along the Soviet border in Lake Khasan in 1938 and at Khalkhin Gol in Manchuria in 1939 clearly revealed the inadequacies of Japanese tank technology and tank tactics when facing a foe equipped to contemporary European standards. The IJA instituted a series of reforms in 1940–41 to update and enlarge their armored force, and the Japanese Kwangtung Army became the focus of efforts to develop a counterweight to the Soviet tank force. In the event, this effort proved to be a temporary diversion when Tokyo shifted the direction of military plans in 1941. After rejecting plans to invade the Soviet Union in concert with Germany in 1941, Tokyo decided to seize the rich resources of the European and American colonies in the Asia–Pacific rim at the end of 1941. The IJA tank regiments formed an armored spearhead for the Japanese offensive operations in the tropical jungles of Singapore, Malaysia, Burma, and the Philippines, and proved remarkably successful in areas long thought to be impassable to tanks.

In spite of these early successes, the IJA tank force stagnated after early 1942. Japanese strategic planning saw little need for tank forces to defend the Pacific islands in its new outer defense belt, and the Imperial Japanese Navy (IJN) was responsible for the Pacific island defenses. The IJA returned to its focus on the China theater, as well as unresolved campaigns in Burma and New Guinea where tank use was restricted by terrain. The armored divisions formed in 1941–42 were primarily oriented towards defending the Manchurian frontier against a potential Soviet incursion. But with the Soviet Union officially neutral, and with enormous demands on Japan's limited industrial resources, tank manufacture was downgraded in priority and neglected through the middle years of the war.

The largest tank-vs-tank battles of the Pacific War were fought in the Philippines in January–February 1945, pitting the Japanese 2nd Armored Division against several US Army tank companies and infantry units. Here, an M4A3 tank named "Classy Peg" of Company C, 716th Tank Battalion, passes a smoldering Type 97-kai Shinhoto Chi-Ha of the Takaki Detachment of the 4th Company, 7th Tank Regiment. The tank had been knocked out during the fighting around Binalonan on January 17, 1945. (NARA)

The principal role for the US Army tank battalions in the Philippines was infantry support. Here, a rifle squad of the 1/161st Infantry move forward behind a tank of the 775th Tank Battalion along Highway 5 during the fighting near Balete Pass on the way to Baguio on March 27, 1945. The 161st Infantry is the same unit that fought with the support of the 716th Tank Battalion at San Manuel two months earlier. One of the problems in tank operations on Luzon was the frequent switch of tank companies from one infantry regiment to another, with no previous joint training and a lack of standardized tactical practices. (NARA)

Japanese tank technology in the 1930s was comparable in quality to European and American tanks, but by 1944 the IJA had fallen woefully behind in design of armored vehicles. This situation was not apparent until much too late. The IJA faced the M3 Stuart light tank in the early Pacific campaigns of 1941–43 and assumed that the US forces would continue to rely on light tanks due to the difficulty in transporting and supporting larger tanks in Pacific conditions. Since the new Type 97-kai Shinhoto Chi-Ha was comparable to the M3 Stuart in performance, there was no apparent need for better tanks.

Both the US Army and US Marine Corps began to deploy the M4 medium tank into the Pacific theater towards the end of 1943, first at Tarawa in November, and subsequently in all of the major campaigns. While the use of medium tanks proved difficult at best in the tropical forests of New Georgia and the Southwest Pacific, the islands of the Central Pacific had coral and volcanic terrain that was much more favorable for tank operations. The Marine Corps began deploying tanks on roughly the same scale as the US Army in Europe, with each division having a supporting tank battalion. The first use of complete Marine medium tank battalions occurred in the summer of 1944 in the Marianas campaign, with the Marines deploying two tank battalions on Saipan in June 1944. Tank–infantry tactics became a hallmark of Marine offensive capability in the final year of the war. Saipan was also the first clash between the M4 Sherman and the Japanese Type 97-kai Shinhoto Chi-Ha. The IJA launched a night counterattack against the US beach-head, the attackers including most of the 9th Tank Regiment, but the attack was shattered. Although the IJA had very weak technical intelligence on the American tank force, by the summer of 1944

the technological imbalance between Japanese and American tanks was becoming painfully clear. It was too late to introduce technological improvements into the Japanese tank force, and in the event, nearly all of the new-generation tanks were hoarded for the final defense of the Japanese Home Islands. Instead, Japanese commanders began to examine new tactics to make their tank units a useful tool in the upcoming island campaigns. This debate was still under way in the autumn of 1944 when the US Army began its campaign to liberate the Philippines.

A photo of the command Shinhoto Chi-Ha on Saipan, the tank of Lt Nishidate, commander of the 3rd Company, 9th Tank Regiment, with the provincial name "Hi-Go" painted on the hull side. (NARA)

CHRONOLOGY

1935

Development of Type 97 Chi-Ha begins.

1938

Production of Type 97 Chi-Ha starts.
Japanese 7th Tank Regiment formed in China.

1939

Work begins on new Japanese 47mm gun based on Nomonhan experience.

May–September   Red Army and Japanese Kwangtung Army fight a series of battles along the Manchurian border called the battle of Khalkhin Gol (Russia) or Nomonhan Incident (Japan); Japanese tank forces defeated.

1941

February   Development of M4 medium tank begins.

December 7–8   Start of the Great Asian War (Japan)/Pacific War (United States).

December   First extensive combat use of Type 97 Chi-Ha in Malaya, Philippines.

1942

January   The commander of the Japanese 7th Tank Regiment requests a crash program to field a 47mm gun version of the Type 97 medium tank.

February   Production of M4A1 medium tank begins.

March   First prototype batch of Type 97-kai Shinhoto Chi-Ha built and shipped to Luzon.

May   Matsuoka Detachment with test batch of Type 97-kai Shinhoto Chi-Ha see combat debut during landings on Corregidor in the Philippines.

June   Japanese 2nd Armored Division formed in Manchuria.

1943

September 20   716th Tank Battalion is formed from the former 3/48th Armored Regiment, 14th Armored Division.

The fighting on Peleliu on September 15, 1944, was another grim reminder of the futility of reflexive counterattacks in the face of overwhelming US firepower advantages. The Tank Company of the 14th Division, with about 15 Type 95 light tanks, charged across the airfield in a daylight attack and was destroyed. (NARA)

1944

February	Production of M4A3 (W) begins.
March	Type 97-kai Shinhoto Chi-Ha production ends.
May	716th Tank Battalion departs United States for New Guinea.
August	Japanese 2nd Armored Division begins departing for Luzon.
December	US Army I Corps departs for Operation *Mike-1* on Luzon.

1945

January 6	Yamashita orders Shigemi Group of 2nd Armored Division to move towards San Manuel.
January 9	I Corps begins amphibious assault in Lingayen Gulf, Luzon.
January 10	716th Tank Battalion supports 43rd Division in push from beach-head.
January 15–16	Takaki Detachment of Shigemi Group makes its first contact with US forces forward of Binalonan.
January 17	Two companies of 7th Tank Regiment, Shigemi Group, are battered at Binalonan and Urdaneta, including fighting with tank platoons of 716th Tank Battalion.
January 19	Company D, 716th Tank Battalion, begins probes of San Manuel defenses.
January 24	Reduction of San Manuel by 161st Regimental Combat Team (RCT) begins.
January 28	Remnants of Shigemi Group retreat after dark from San Manuel towards St Nicolas.
January 29	San Manuel declared secure by 161st RCT.

A Type 97-kai of the 3rd Company, 7th Tank Regiment knocked out in Binalonan during the fighting on January 17, is inspected the next day by technical intelligence troops of Depot Team 3. (NARA)

DESIGN AND DEVELOPMENT

TYPE 97-KAI SHINHOTO CHI-HA MEDIUM TANK

The Type 97 Chi-Ha was developed in the mid 1930s as a replacement for the older Type 89 Chi-Ro medium tank. The origins of these tanks are covered in more detail in the Osprey New Vanguard series, and the focus here instead will be on the improved version of the Chi-Ha series, the Type 97-kai Shinhoto Chi-Ha.[1] The basic version of the Chi-Ha went into production in 1938 and it was comparable to many of the medium tanks of its era, such as the Soviet BT-7, Italian M-11/39, and Vickers 6-ton tank derivatives such as the Soviet T-26 and Polish 7TP. Japanese tank design was shaped by the tactical demands in the IJA's principal theater of operations in China, so its tanks were light and lightly armored, and the Chi-Ha's 57mm gun was oriented towards its infantry-support role rather than for tank-vs-tank fighting.

The Chinese Army had very few tanks and its antitank arsenal was equally paltry. The Chi-Ha saw its combat debut in May 1939 when four of the new tanks, part of Lt Gen Masaomi Yasuoka's 1st Tank Group, saw combat with the Red Army along the Halka River (Khalkhin Gol in Russian) in Manchuria in the "Nomonhan Incident." The IJA armor in this skirmish was substantially outnumbered by the Red Army tank force, and the fighting went very badly for the Japanese, with 42 of the 73 tanks of

---

1. See Steven J. Zaloga, *Japanese Tanks 1939–45*, New Vanguard 137, Oxford, Osprey (2007)

The combat debut of the Type 97-kai Shinhoto Chi-Ha took place at Corregidor in May 1942 with the Matsuoka Detachment, a special unit formed at the Chiba Tank School to rush the new type into service. Two of the detachment's tanks are seen here during the 1942 fighting on Luzon. (Tom Laemlein)

the 1st Tank Group knocked out in July 1939. Most of the Japanese tanks were destroyed by the Soviet 45mm gun, which had far better range and penetration than Japanese weapons; this weapon was used both as a towed antitank gun as well as the armament of Soviet armored vehicles such as the BT-7 cavalry tank and BA-10 armored car.

The poor performance of Japanese tanks in Manchuria in 1939 led to an effort to field a more effective medium tank with performance similar to or better than that of the Soviet BT-7. The centerpiece of the modernization program was the new Type 1 47mm gun. This was developed both as a towed antitank gun and as a tank gun to replace the 57mm gun on the Chi-Ha tank. Besides the development of the new gun, a substantial redesign of the Type 97 Chi-Ha tank was undertaken as the Type 1 Chi-He. The maximum armor thickness of the Type 97 was only 30mm making it vulnerable to the Soviet 45mm gun, so the frontal armor on the Chi-He was thickened to 50mm. The front glacis plate was simplified using a straight, flat plate, and more extensive use of welding was introduced to reduce the risk of rivets being shattered inward if hit in combat. To accommodate the added weight, the improved Type 100 diesel engine was developed which offered 240hp compared to the 170hp of the earlier versions. This design was accepted for production in 1941, but in the event, other events transpired which delayed the start of production.

The Type 97 Chi-Ha tank was used extensively in the 1941 Operation *Centrifuge* offensive in Malaya and the Philippines. During this fighting, the IJA confronted the US Army's new M3 Stuart light tank for the first time when fighting against British forces in Burma and against the US Army in the Philippines. Once again, Japanese tank guns were shown to be inadequate against the enemy tanks. Col Seinosuke Sonoda, the commander of the Japanese 7th Tank Regiment on Luzon in the Philippines, had served before the campaign with the Tank Research Committee of the Army Ministry, and was well aware of the new 47mm tank gun. He placed a special request to Tokyo to expedite the delivery of a 47mm tank to the Philippines as quickly as possible. This request was transmitted to the Sagami Army Arsenal, which was Japan's primary tank development center, and in turn the request was forwarded to the Mitsubishi Jukogyo Company Ltd, which was preparing prototypes of the Type 1 Chi-He tank for serial production at their Tokyo-Kiki factory. Since the Type 1 was not ready for such production, the Mitsubishi plant modified the basic Type 97 medium tank chassis to accept the larger Type 1 turret with 47mm gun and ten tanks were converted. A special company was formed under Major Matsuoka from troops of the 2nd Tank Regiment and hastily trained on the new tanks at the Chiba tank school. The Matsuoka Detachment arrived in the Philippines on March 29, 1942, but Matsuoka was transferred to the command of the 7th Tank Regiment on April 6 after Sonoda had been killed.

By this stage, most of the fighting on Luzon had ended, but the Japanese 14th Army planned an assault on the last American bastion on Corregidor in May 1942

TYPE 97-KAI SHINHOTO CHI-HA TANK, 7TH TANK REGIMENT, 2ND ARMORED DIVISION

Length: 5.5m

Width: 2.33m

Height: 2.38m

Weight: 14.8 metric tons (empty); 15.8 metric tons (combat loaded)

Armor (hull): 17mm (glacis); 25mm (front plate); 20mm (side superstructure)

Armor (turret): 25mm (turret front); 30mm (gun mantlet)

Main gun: Type 1 47mm gun

Elevation: −8 to +10 degrees

Ammunition: 104 47mm rounds

Sight: Type 1 telescopic sight

Secondary armament: Two Type 97 7.7mm machine guns

Ammunition: 2,575 7.7mm rounds

Engine: 170hp air-cooled V-12 diesel

Transmission: Clutch-brake steering with 4F+1R gear box

Max. speed: 38km/h

Range: 210km

5.5m

and wanted tank support. The Matsuoka Detachment, led by Capt Hideo Ho, was assigned the task. Curiously enough, Ho led the attack in a captured American M3 light tank. Five of the new Type 97-kai medium tanks and the captured M3 light tank landed during the first wave around midnight on May 5–6, 1942. The tanks had considerable difficulty surmounting the rocky shore, but eventually crested the beach and began to grind through the American defenses. The tanks were instrumental in silencing several American defensive positions and a Japanese after-action account noted that they proved "more effective than anticipated." The US garrison surrendered on May 6, ending the first Philippines campaign.

The improvised Type 97-kai design, also called the Shinhoto Chi-Ha (New Turret Chi-Ha) came at an awkward moment in the Japanese tank program. The Nomonhan Incident had convinced the IJA of the need to expand its tank force, and the 1939 plan anticipated increasing tank production from its 1939 level of about 500 annually to 1,200 tanks per year. At the time, the tank effort was given the A1 classification of industrial priority. The Type 97 had initially been in production at three plants: the Sagami Army Arsenal, Mitsubishi's Tokyo-Kiki factory, and Hitachi's Kameari factory, so four more plants were added in early 1942 to increase the output. No sooner had this begun than the War Ministry was reconsidering industrial priorities. Having conquered a vast new empire, the IJA and IJN now faced the prospects of having to defend the conquests against American and British counterattacks. As a result, offensive weapons such as tanks were deemed less important for future defensive operations than warships and combat aircraft. In addition, the principal role for the IJA tank force had been to act as a counterweight against the Red Army in Manchuria. Since the War Ministry had rejected plans to invade the Soviet Union in concert with Germany, the plan to form ten tank divisions was substantially cut. In consequence,

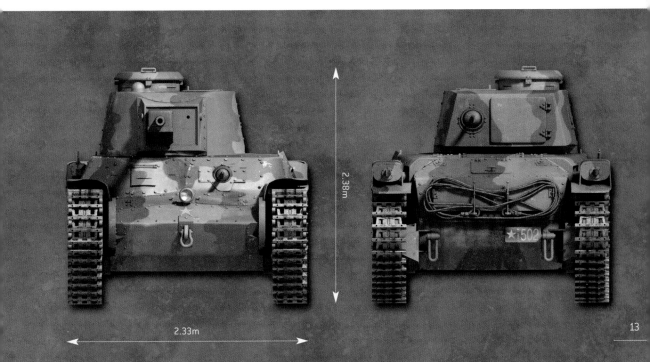

2.38m

2.33m

The Type 97-kai began appearing in combat in increasing numbers in 1944. This is a Type 97-kai of the 14th Tank Regiment in Burma during the disastrous Imphal campaign in the spring of 1944, when the regiment lost most of its tanks. (NARA)

the industrial priority for tank production fell from A1 to D. As a fraction of Japanese ordnance production, tank production slipped from 26 percent of the annual production in 1941 to only 11 percent by 1944.

Under these circumstances, manufacture of the new and more expensive Type 1 tank was reconsidered. The production of the Type 97-kai was a less expensive option, which required no re-tooling. It offered the same increased firepower as the Type 1, even if not the armor protection. In addition, the older Type 97 could be rebuilt in the Shinhoto Chi-Ha configuration by adding the new turret to existing tanks. As a result, the Type 1 production program was delayed until February 1944, and in the event only 170 were built. A total of 400 of the new Type 1 47mm tank gun were ordered in fiscal year 1942 and they entered production in April 1942. Through most of 1942, the Type 97-kai was produced alongside the existing Type 97 until 47mm gun production caught up with the tank production, which finally occurred in April 1943. Data on how many Type 97-kai were manufactured is not available from remaining records. A total of 958 Chi-Ha tanks were manufactured from April 1942, when 47mm tank gun production began, until March 1944 when

American forces began encountering the Shinhoto Chi-Ha during the Marianas campaign in the summer of 1944. This was the regimental command tank of Lt Col Tadashi Goshima of the 9th Tank Regiment, with the regiment's usual dashed command band and the name "Aso" (Japan's largest volcano) painted on the hull side. There were only four of these Shinhoto Chi-Ha on Saipan. (NARA)

production ended at Hitachi. However, only 272 47mm guns were manufactured in 1942 compared to 366 Chi-Ha tanks in April–December 1942, so Type 97-kai Shinhoto Chi-Ha production may have been around 860 tanks. Records on the conversion of the older Type 97 to the Type 97-kai are also incomplete, but the evidence would suggest that about 115 were completed, mainly in 1945.

The IJA learned of advances in tank technology through military attachés in Germany, and samples of the PzKpfw III and Tiger tank were ordered. Captured examples of the Soviet T-34 and American M4 Sherman were examined by Japanese officers in Germany. The Type 3 Chi-Nu was developed, armed with a 75mm gun, but production did not start until late in 1944, and both the Type 1 Chi-He and Type 3 Chi-Nu were reserved for the final defense of the Japanese Home Islands. So the Type 97-kai Shinhoto Chi-Ha remained the best Japanese tank to see combat service in the Pacific in 1945.

The Japanese 1st and 2nd Companies, 9th Tank Regiment, were detached to the garrison on neighboring Guam. This is the command tank of Lt Kumagaya who led the 2nd Company, and the tank was the only Shinhoto Chi-Ha on Guam. It has the regiment's command band around the turret and a very prominent star marking. (NARA)

M4A3 MEDIUM TANK

The M4A3 medium tank employed by the 716th Tank Battalion on Luzon was a heavily modified version of the tank that originally appeared in 1942. The US Army did not distinguish production batches of its tanks like Britain (Mark I, Mk. II, etc.) or Germany (Ausfuhrung A, Ausf. B, etc.), which makes this distinction less apparent. In fact, the M4A3 seen on Luzon had little in common with the first Sherman tanks that saw their combat debut at El Alamein in the summer of 1942.

The M4 series of tanks was developed in 1941 as a replacement for the stop-gap M3 medium tank series and production began in February 1942. American tank production was given less priority than aircraft production and so the Sherman had to make do with whatever engines were available, instead of relying on a single type. So the many sub-variants of the Sherman were distinguished mainly by engine types: the welded-hull M4 and cast-hull M4A1 with a Continental radial aircraft engine; M4A2 with twin truck diesels; the M4A3 with a Ford GAA in-line gasoline aircraft engine; and the M4A4 with a Chrysler bus engine combination in a star pattern. Although "Sherman" was a British name for the M4 family and not used by the US Army in World War II, it will be used here for convenience.

Combat in 1942–43 revealed two principal shortcomings of the Sherman – armor protection and main armament fire controls. The Sherman had much of its ammunition stowed in bins in the sponsons over the tracks. As a result, when the hull armor was penetrated either on the front corners or on the forward parts of the hull side, there was a very high probability that the ammunition would be hit and set on fire. One of the more prevalent myths about the Sherman was that its propensity to fire was due to its use of a gasoline engine. Operational research into tank casualties in 1942–43 found this to be false, and the main problem was the high probability of an ammunition fire if the tank armor was penetrated. The ammunition propellant was very susceptible to fire, and once a single round of ammunition was ignited it was virtually impossible to extinguish, leading to a catastrophic chain reaction with neighboring ammunition that would incinerate the tank.

Since it was unlikely that the Sherman would ever be armored sufficiently to resist all potential enemy projectiles without becoming excessively heavy, a major effort was

M4A3(W) MEDIUM TANK, COMPANY C, 716TH TANK BATTALION

Length: 20.6ft

Width: 8.75ft

Height: 9.6ft

Weight: 34.8 tons combat loaded (31.5 tons unloaded)

Ground pressure: 14.3psi

Armor (hull): 2.5in (front); 1.5in (side); 1.0in (floor); 0.5in (rear)

Armor (turret): 3.5in (gun shield); 3.0in (front); 2.0in (sides); 1.0in (top)

Main gun: 75mm M3 gun in M34A1 mount

Elevation: −10 to +25 degrees

Traverse: 360 degrees in 15 seconds (hydraulic)

Ammunition: 104 rounds

Sight: M71D telescope, M4A1 periscope

Secondary armament: .30cal co-axial, .30cal hull mount

Ammunition: 6,250 rounds

Engine: Ford GAA 8-cylinder. 4-cycle gasoline, 500hp @ 2,600rpm

Transmission: Syncromesh 5F+1R

Max. speed: 26mph

Range: 100 miles

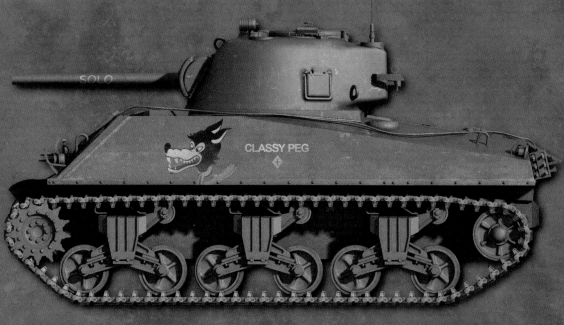

CLASSY PEG

20.6ft

made to reduce the probability of ammunition fires. The eventual solution was called "wet stowage." This had two key elements. The most important aspect of this program was to move the ammunition from the vulnerable location in the sponsons to the floor underneath the turret. The main advantage of moving the ammunition was that it was far less likely to be hit. The second aspect of the program was to locate the ammunition in lightly armored bins. This was not intended to protect the ammunition from a direct hit by a large-caliber antitank projectile, but rather to shield it from splinters or shrapnel, which could ignite the ammunition propellant. To reduce further the probability of the ammunition being ignited by a hot piece of shrapnel or other fiery debris, the ammunition bins contained an outer shell that could be filled with water or antifreeze. An Army study in 1945 concluded that only 10–15 percent of the wet-stowage Shermans burned when penetrated in combat compared to 60–80 percent of the older dry-stowage Shermans.

The "wet stowage" features became available in late 1943 at the same time that other hull improvements were being made. There had been complaints that the driver and co-driver hatches on the front of the hull were too small to permit rapid exit in combat, so new enlarged hatches were developed. These required a reconfiguration of the hull glacis plate and the redesign also provided an opportunity to simplify

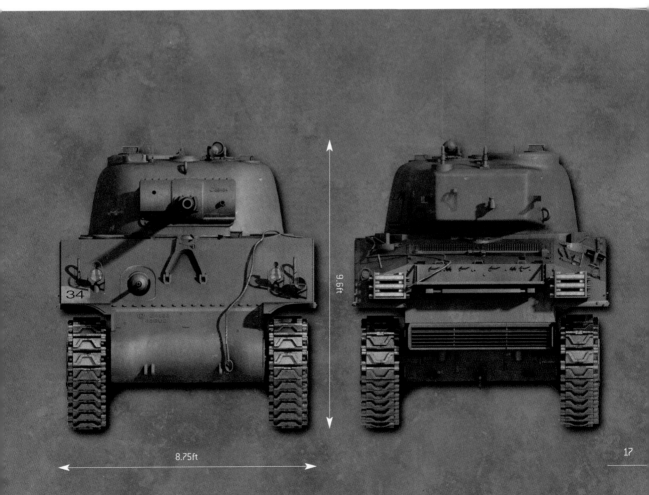

9.6ft

8.75ft

Japan developed more substantial tanks late in the war, such as the Type 3 Chi-Nu, armed with a 75mm gun. However, only 144 were built, production starting in September 1944, and they were all reserved for the final defense of the Home Islands. (NARA)

manufacture by introducing single plate construction instead of the complicated design of the early Shermans, which had prominent bulges to accommodate the driver/co-driver hatches. This hull configuration is sometimes called the "47-degree hull" due to the angle of the new glacis plate, or "big hatch hull" due to the enlarged hatches. Another hull improvement in the latter half of 1943 was the improved one-piece differential housing – the large casting at the front of the lower hull that covered the transmission. The new design improved ballistic protection and it entered production at various plants from June to September 1943. In the case of the M4A3, the new hull configuration with the wet-stowage features was introduced as a package in February 1944. As a result, the production of this particular version of the Sherman was beginning just as Type 97-kai Shinhoto Chi-Ha production was ending.

While these various hull improvements were under way, a number of turret improvements were also being introduced. The early Shermans relied on a periscopic sight for the gunner that was mechanically linked to the gun mount. The British Army was very critical of this configuration, since the alignment between the periscopic sight and the gun mount could be easily knocked about, decreasing gun accuracy. The solution was the introduction of a telescopic sight. This sight required a modification of the M34 gun mount, and the resulting version with the telescopic sight was adopted as the M34A1 in February–March 1943.

Combat revealed that the turret casting on early Shermans had a weak spot in front of the gunner on the right side. The deficit was initially addressed by welding a curved piece of appliqué armor over the area; this work began in August 1943. A more satisfactory solution was to change the casting so that the armor was thickened in this spot. The new "large hatch" hull required other turret changes, such as increasing the clearance under the rear turret bustle to provide enough clearance for the hatch. Another shortcoming of the early turret design was the provision of only a single escape hatch on the turret roof over the commander. In the event that the commander was

incapacitated, it became difficult for the gunner and loader to escape. As a result, a second hatch was added over the loader's station on the right side of the turret. A new turret basket was also necessary to accommodate the wet stowage below the turret. These various features were incorporated into the definitive version of the 75mm gun turret, the D78461 in September 1943, more often called the "high bustle" turret. This turret was used on the new M4A3 with wet stowage, and Ordnance documents called this version of tank the M4A3W or M4A3(W), with the "W" indicating wet stowage. The M4A3W designation was not widely used in the Army outside official internal Ordnance documents.

The M4A3 was used by the 716th Tank Battalion in the Luzon battles described later, but this was not the only, nor the most common, Sherman variant in the Philippines. Most Army tank battalions in the Philippines used late-production M4 medium tanks, sometimes called "composite hull" tanks due to their unusual hull

The most common version of the Sherman in Army use in the Philippines was the late-production M4 with the composite hull. As can be seen, the front of the hull has the cast shape more commonly associated with the M4A1, but the rest of the hull is the usual welded construction. This is an instruction course at the Composite Unit Combat Training Center – Pacific on Oahu in January 1945. (NARA)

The M4 (105mm) assault gun resembled a normal tank but was armed with a 105mm howitzer instead of the normal 75mm gun. It can be distinguished both by its thicker barrel and a slightly different gun mantlet. This is an assault gun of the 44th Tank Battalion that was ambushed 15 miles behind the lines during the fighting in the Cagayen Valley of Luzon between the 37th Division and the Japanese 2nd Armored Division in June 1945. (NARA)

construction. In 1943, Ordnance decided to simplify the production of the normal M4 glacis plate, which had been made of several pieces of rolled armor plate and cast armor parts that were welded together. This configuration was complicated to assemble and potentially more vulnerable to enemy fire. One solution was simply to adopt the front of the cast M4A1 hull. The M4 composite hull consisted of a cast front end welded to a normal M4 welded hull. The option was selected prior to the adoption of the new big-hatch 47-degree hull as used on the M4A3W. Yet only a limited number of the small-hatch composite M4 hulls were manufactured before switching to the large-hatch M4A1 front. This version of the M4 with the composite large-hatch hull was by far the most common Sherman type in the Philippines. In general, Army tank battalions in the Pacific standardized on a single Sherman type and did not mix M4 and M4A3 in the same battalion, as was often the case in the European theater.

Two new armament options for the Sherman became available around the same time as the wet-stowage versions: a 76mm gun and a 105mm howitzer. The 76mm gun was introduced to provide better antitank firepower. This version was not deployed to the Pacific theater so it will be ignored here.[2] The 105mm howitzer was adopted on an assault-gun version of the Sherman tank. It was already in use on the Sherman chassis as the M7 105mm HMC (howitzer motor carriage), which served in armored field artillery battalions. The assault-gun version used a related weapon, but mounted in a conventional tank turret instead of an open casemate. It was intended to provide direct and indirect fire support in the tank battalions, and was not intended for the field artillery. Under the new 1943 tables of organization and equipment (TO&E), the tank battalions had a platoon of three assault guns in the headquarters company and one assault gun in each of the three medium tank companies, for a total of six assault guns per battalion. The assault guns closely resembled the normal 75mm gun tanks, though they can be distinguished by a slightly different gun mantlet, a shorter and stubbier gun barrel, and the provision of an extra fan on the turret roof to deal with the greater volume of cordite fumes generated inside the turret by the howitzer. The assault-gun versions of the Sherman did not begin appearing in the European theater until July 1944, but some units in the Pacific, such as the 716th Tank Battalion, were issued with this vehicle as standard equipment. Curiously enough, the first production version of the 105mm assault gun was built on the M4 chassis, but with the large-hatch welded hull, not the composite hull so prevalent on the 75mm gun tank versions of the late M4.

---

2. See Steven J. Zaloga, *Panther vs Sherman: Battle of the Bulge 1944*, Duel 13, Oxford, Osprey (2008) and Steven J. Zaloga, *M4 (76mm) Sherman Medium Tank 1943–65*, New Vanguard 73, Oxford, Osprey (2003)

TECHNICAL
SPECIFICATIONS

FIREPOWER

The M4A3 had an overwhelming firepower advantage against the Type 97-kai since its 75mm gun could penetrate the Japanese tank at any normal combat range, while the Japanese tank gun was only effective against the Sherman in frontal engagements at very close ranges of about 150–200 yards, or against the Sherman's weaker side armor.

The Type 97-kai Shinhoto Chi-Ha was armed with a Type 1 47mm tank gun. Two types of ammunition were available for the gun: the Type 1 high-explosive (HE) projectile and the Type 1 armor-piercing/high-explosive (APHE) projectile. The APHE round could penetrate 67–75mm of vertical armor at 500 yards or 53–60mm of armor at 30 degrees at 500 yards. The M4A3W had front armor of 63mm at 47 degrees, and turret front armor of 89mm. As a result, the Type 1 gun was not capable of penetrating the Sherman at normal combat ranges, and would either have to engage it at point-blank range or fire against its thinner side armor. Japanese tankers were instructed to hold their fire as long as possible. During one of the Luzon engagements, an M4A3 was hit six times by 47mm APHE at ranges from 150 to 200 yards and suffered five complete penetrations and one partial penetration.

One drawback of switching from the original Type 97 57mm gun on the baseline Type 97 Chi-Ha tank to the newer Type 1 47mm gun was the inadequate HE firepower of the 47mm projectile when used against targets other than tanks. The 57mm gun

The gunner's station in the Type 97-kai, viewed through the roof hatch. The five ready rounds are evident to the left, the traversing wheel is in the center, and the 47mm Type 1 gun is to the right. (NARA)

fired the Type 90 HE projectile, which had a high-explosive fill of 0.55lb; the Type 1 shell had only about a third the high-explosive fill (0.19lb).

The Type 97-kai tank carried 104 rounds of 47mm ammunition; a typical ammunition load for the Type 97-kai on Luzon was 66 rounds of APHE and 38 rounds of HE. There were five ready rounds on the right and left side of the turret front, and a 30-round bin in the right turret bustle. The two main hull stores were a 30-round bin in the left rear corner behind the loader, and four smaller bins above the power train and in the sponsons.

The Type 97-kai had two 7.7mm Type 97 machine guns. One was placed in a ball-mount in the left front hull for use by the bow machine-gunner, while the other was placed in a ball-mount in the left rear of the turret, where it was operated by the loader. There was no co-axial machine gun adjacent to the main gun. Either of the two hull machine guns could be dismounted and used as an antiaircraft machine gun via a simple pintle mount on the turret roof.

The M4A3 was armed with an M3 75mm gun. The gunner could aim the weapon either with an M70F telescopic sight or the M4A1 periscopic sight. Turret traverse was much faster than on the Type 97, since a hydraulic turret traverse system was available. Tanks usually carried the M61 75mm armor-piercing-capped (APC), M48 HE, and M64 white phosphorus smoke rounds. The M61 APC round could penetrate the Type 97-kai tank at any normal combat range. The 75mm HE round was also much more effective than that of the 47mm gun, with a bursting charge of 1.47lb, which was seven times greater than that of the Japanese round. The M4A3 carried 104 rounds of ammunition, mainly in armored bins under the floor, and with an eight-round ready-rack on the turret basket floor.

The M4A3 had a more extensive assortment of secondary armament than the Shinhoto Chi-Ha, including a .30cal hull machine gun, a .30cal co-axial machine gun, and an externally mounted .50cal heavy machine gun for antiaircraft defense; some tanks had a 2in M3 mortar fitted in the left corner of the turret for firing smoke.

Table 1. Armor penetration, 47mm vs 75mm guns		
Vertical armor	500 yards	1,000 yards
Japanese 47mm APHE	67mm	55mm
US 75mm M61 APC	74–86mm*	66–79mm*
* Difference due to homogenous vs face-hardened plate		

PROTECTION

The M4A3 Sherman had substantially better armored protection than the Type 97-kai Shinhoto Chi-Ha; the Sherman was proof against most Japanese antitank weapons except at close ranges, while the Shinhoto Chi-Ha was vulnerable to the Sherman as well as to most US infantry antitank weapons.

Besides being vulnerable to the 75mm gun of the M4A3, the thin armor of the Shinhoto Chi-Ha also left it exposed to a wide range of US infantry antitank weapons. Indeed, more tanks of the Japanese 2nd Armored Division were lost to infantry weapons than to tank-gun fire. The standard US Army infantry antitank gun in 1944 was the 57mm M1. Japanese tank armor was so weak that most infantry units in the Pacific theater retained the older 37mm M3 gun, since it was much lighter (950lb vs 2,810lb) and so much easier to handle by its crew. Each infantry battalion had an antitank platoon with three guns, usually the 37mm gun, while each regiment had an additional antitank company with nine guns and these were sometimes the larger and heavier 57mm weapon. The 37mm gun could penetrate 61mm of armor at 500 yards, which was more than adequate to penetrate the Shinhoto Chi-Ha.

A more numerous antitank weapon was the 2.36in rocket launcher, better known as the bazooka. There were 112 of these in each rifle regiment, mainly issued to headquarters and artillery units for antitank defense. During fighting in the Pacific, where there was so little threat from Japanese tanks, they were often collected and issued to rifle companies and platoons for more offensive employment. Such was the case with the 161st Infantry, as will be described later, which made extensive use of bazookas for tank-hunting during the battle for San Manuel. The bazooka could easily penetrate the armor of the Shinhoto Chi-Ha if its warhead detonated properly, but its main fault was an erratic fuze, which often caused the rocket to ricochet off the tank without detonating.

Another weapon widely used in the Philippines fighting was the M9A1 antitank rifle grenade. This could be fired from standard rifles and carbines using a special blank cartridge and adapter. The grenades were widely used in the Luzon fighting, and tests conducted on captured tanks after the campaign found that they were effective at ranges up to 75 yards and would punch a half-inch hole through the Shinhoto Chi-Ha armor. In some cases, US troops used .50cal heavy machine guns against the Shinhoto Chi-Ha. This was a weapon of last resort, and could sometimes penetrate the lower side armor at very short ranges of 35–50 yards, or score lucky penetrations through weak spots such as the machine-gun ball mounts.

Although there are no comprehensive statistics available, it would appear that most

Table 2. Comparative armor thickness

	Type 97-kai	M4A3W
Turret front	33mm at 0 degrees	89mm curved
Turret sides	26mm at 11 degrees	51mm at 5 degrees
Hull glacis	25mm at 11 degrees	64mm at 47 degrees
Lower hull	20mm at 30 degrees	51–114mm curved
Hull side	26mm at 25 degrees	38mm at 0 degrees

Although the 47mm gun of the Type 97-kai could not reliably penetrate the frontal armor of a Sherman tank at longer combat ranges, it was very effective against the M4's side armor, as is evident from this M4A3, which has been penetrated multiple times through the side during the January 1945 fighting. (NARA)

Sherman tank losses in combat during the fighting with the 2nd Armored Division were caused by direct-fire weapons, especially the 47mm tank and antitank guns. As mentioned earlier, the 47mm gun could reliably penetrate Sherman side armor, so Japanese tankers and antitank gun crews were encouraged to use their weapons from ambush positions so that they could fire on the sides or rear of American tanks. The IJA had armor-piercing ammunition available in 75mm caliber – the Type 1 AP round which could penetrate about 90mm of vertical armor at 500 yards. There is little evidence this was used extensively in the Philippines for tank fighting, however. The 75mm Type 90 field gun was capable of disabling the Sherman tank with normal HE strikes to the tracks and suspension, which caused mobility kills.

In most Pacific campaigns of 1944–45, the main threats to American tanks were mines and close-attack infantry weapons.[3] (These were not a significant factor in the fighting with the 2nd Armored Division in northern Luzon, as there were so few infantry there.) An American assessment of Japanese mine warfare in the Philippines considered the equipment and doctrine to be sound, but the actual employment of mines to be inadequate and often inept. The one innovation in infantry antitank weapons in the Philippines was the introduction of the lunge mine, one of a number of new suicide weapons introduced in 1944. This weapon was a shaped-charge warhead mounted on a long pole, and an infantryman would wait in ambush, then run up to the tank and press the warhead against the tank and detonate the charge. At least one M7 105mm HMC was knocked out in the San Manuel fighting by this weapon.

MOBILITY

The M4A3 and Type 97-kai had similar mobility, with no particular advantage to either type. The M4A3, although double the weight of the Shinhoto Chi-Ha, had a much more powerful engine and was slightly faster. The Shinhoto Chi-Ha had marginally better range, and due to its lighter weight it could move more confidently across soft ground.

---

3. For more detail on the US Marines' experience with Japanese antitank tactics in 1944–45, see Steven J. Zaloga, *US Marine Corps Tanks of WWII*, New Vanguard 186, Oxford, Osprey (2012)

Table 3. Comparative performance		
	M4A3W	Type 97-kai
Combat weight (tons)	34.8	17.4
Engine	Ford GAA	Mitsubishi SA 12200VD
Horsepower	450	170
Horsepower/weight ratio (hp/ton)	12.9	9.7
Road speed (mph)	26	24
Range (miles)	100	130
Ground pressure (psi)	14.3	8.7

COMMAND AND CONTROL

The gunner on the Type 97-kai had a telescopic sight offering a 4× magnification. While this optic was certainly an adequate tank sight, the lack of a periscopic sight meant that the gunner had no view of the terrain and so no situational awareness. The commander would select the target either while observing from outside the tank, or while sitting protected from inside the tank. The Type 97-kai had provision for a monocular, rotating periscopic sight for the commander that could be fitted under a small hemispheric dome located either in front of the cupola or mounted in the

The most potent antitank weapon available to Japanese infantry units was the 47mm Type 1 antitank gun, which entered production in April 1942 and began seeing widespread deployment in the Pacific theater in the summer of 1944, such as at Saipan. Here is a camouflaged example on Peleliu. (NARA)

overhead hatch, depending on the production batch. However, few tanks actually received these devices in 1944 because of the general austerity measures that plagued the tank industry. Instead, the tank commander had to rely on the vision devices in the cupola if operating from inside the tank. The cupola had a total of six vision devices, five of these being ordinary protectoscopes (view slits covered by three-ply armored glass) and a single periscopic sight at the front.

Japanese tank units issued tank radios only to platoon and company commanders. The most common set in 1944 was the Vehicle Radio Set Type C Mark 1 (Model

The Type 97-kai was
vulnerable to a wide range
of weapons, including the US
infantry's 2.36in "bazooka"
rocket launcher. This bazooka
team of Sgt John Milkem and
Pfc David Damschen of the
27th Infantry was credited
with knocking out a Type
97-kai Shinhoto Chi-Ha of Capt
Shoji Arao's 2nd Company,
6th Tank Regiment, on the
night of January 29–30 along
the Pemienta–Umingan
section of Highway 8. (NARA)

305) and it was fitted in a container behind the bow machine-gunner. This was a transmitter–receiver with a transmitting power of 6 watts, and could be used in either voice or telegraphic mode, with an effective range of about a third of a mile in voice mode and about 6 miles in telegraphic mode. Allied intelligence assessments of the radio found it to be extremely sturdy and well made, but of low power, too dependent on fixed-frequency crystals, and using a microphone poorly suited to internal tank use. In the event, Japanese tank tactics in the Philippines did not encourage the use of the radio for fear that conversations would be monitored by US signals intelligence units. Communications between tanks in a platoon used signal flags or runners.

The M4A3 had a more sophisticated set of fire controls than the Type 97-kai. The gunner had two devices to aim the gun: a unitary M4A1 periscope with an integrated M38A2 telescopic sight, and a co-axial M70F telescope with 5× magnification. The advantage of having both a periscopic sight and a telescopic sight was that the gunner could view the terrain through the periscope while approaching the objective, and so develop good situational awareness as well as assisting the tank commander in searching

The Type 97-kai tank commander had a vision cupola over his station with six protected view slots. This photo, taken from the gunner's station towards the commander's station, also shows the commander's traverse wheel and the small pistol port on the right side of the turret. (Author)

for likely targets. In the event that a snap-firing solution had to be made, the gunner could aim the gun through the periscopic sight due to its incorporation of the telescopic sight with aiming reticles. For a more precise aim, he could switch to the main telescopic sight.

The vision devices available to the tank commander varied from tank to tank. The US Army was in the process of switching from the original two-piece split hatch to a new all-vision cupola for the tank commander. The initial type had provisions for a standard M6 periscope or a 7× periscopic binocular sight. The all-vision cupola had six laminated-glass vision ports for all-around vision and had the usual periscope fitting. The newer all-vision cupola was not approved until April 1944, so a large proportion of the M4A3 tanks in service in the Philippines had the older hatch configuration, which was inferior to the Type 97-kai in terms of the view from under-armor protection.

US tank units had a more ample distribution of radios, and the radios were of better quality and higher power than the Japanese equivalents. In a standard tank platoon, the platoon leader and the platoon sergeant had the SCR-528, which included a transmitter and a receiver. The other three tanks had the SCR-538, which was only a receiver. The Sherman used FM radios, which were less susceptible to interference than the AM radios used on the Type 97-kai.

TYPE 97-KAI TURRET

1   Type 97 7.7mm light machine gun
2   Gunner's shoulder rest
3   Gunner's turret traverse wheel
4   Gunner's side 47mm ready ammunition rack
5   Gunner's hatch
6   Gunner's Type 1 telescopic sight
7   Type 1 47mm tank gun
8   Tank commander's hatch
9   Commander's vision sight
10 Commander's side 47mm ready ammunition rack
11 Rear turret ammunition stowage bin

12 Japanese Type 1 47mm Armor-piercing round
13 Japanese Type 1 47mm High-explosive round

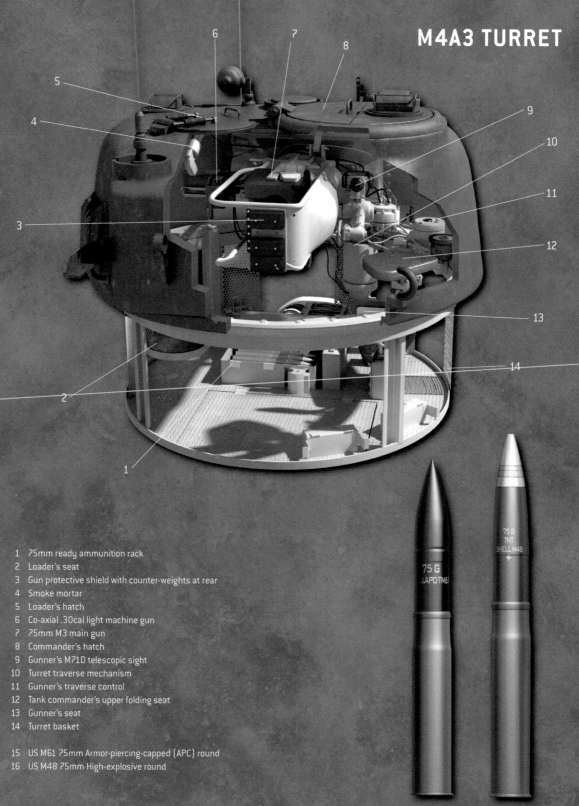

M4A3 TURRET

1 75mm ready ammunition rack
2 Loader's seat
3 Gun protective shield with counter-weights at rear
4 Smoke mortar
5 Loader's hatch
6 Co-axial .30cal light machine gun
7 75mm M3 main gun
8 Commander's hatch
9 Gunner's M71D telescopic sight
10 Turret traverse mechanism
11 Gunner's traverse control
12 Tank commander's upper folding seat
13 Gunner's seat
14 Turret basket

15 US M61 75mm Armor-piercing-capped (APC) round
16 US M48 75mm High-explosive round

75 G
J.APC-TM61

75 G
TNT
SHELL M48

15   16

THE COMBATANTS

JAPANESE TANK CREW

The Type 97-kai had a conventional layout with a crew of five. The turret crew consisted of the tank commander on the right side seated below the vision cupola, the gunner in the front left side of the turret, and the loader behind the gunner in the left side. The crew in the hull consisted of a driver on the right side in front of the commander and the bow-machine gunner to the left. The crew responsibilities were conventional, with the commander directing the crew and selecting targets for the gunner. The main gun could be traversed manually by either the gunner or commander, who both had traversing wheels. Usually the commander selected the target and roughly traversed the turret to the proper orientation, while instructing the gunner of the target, and then the gunner performed the fine adjustments.

The Type 97-kai had little room inside, even allowing for the fact that Japanese tankers tended to be of smaller stature than Americans. The turret was especially cramped. One interesting innovation on Japanese tanks was the extensive use of thin sheets of asbestos attached to key parts of the turret and hull walls, to provide a slight amount of relief from the hot metal of the tank in tropical conditions.

Japanese tank company commanders were usually captains or first lieutenants, while platoon commanders were typically second lieutenants or warrant officers. The remaining tanks in the platoon were commanded by warrant officers or sergeants. A typical medium tank company in the 7th Tank Regiment in 1945 had 12 tanks consisting of 11 Type 97 medium tanks and one Type 95 light tank. The HQ section had the commander's tank, the HQ section leader's tank, and the single Type 95, which was used for scouting or other assignments. Each of the three platoons had three tanks each.

Early in the war, Japanese tank units had preferential selection from Army draftees, favoring young men with driving licenses and high-school education. After basic training, tankers were usually sent to specialist schools or directly to their units, where specialized training took place. The IJA established the Chiba Tank School in 1936 and later expanded the network with a Mechanics' Tank School and a Maintenance School in 1941. With the expansion of the tank force in Manchuria after the Nomonhan Incident, the Kungchuling Tank School was established in Manchuria in December 1940, moving to Siping in 1942. The IJA tankers' training was thorough, and the standard practice was to cross-train crews so that each crewman had at least a basic understanding of every task on the tank to keep the vehicle operating in the event of casualties. Ammunition was plentiful, so gunnery training was extensive. Maneuver training was quite limited due to fuel shortages, so exercises above company level were relatively rare.

From available records, it is unclear how many, if any, of the 7th Tank Regiment's tankers were veterans of the 1941–42 campaign on Luzon. A quick biographical sketch of a few tankers from the 2nd Armored Division will help give a sense of typical career paths. Sgt Y. Aoyama was drafted in February 1941 and sent to Koun, Manchuria, where he trained with the 43rd Infantry Regiment. After training, he was assigned to the 3rd Border Garrison in Manchuria. In September 1943, he was promoted and sent to the 10th Tank Regiment in Tungan, also in Manchuria, where he was re-trained as a tank driver.

Cpl I. Shirayama was recruited in January 1942 and sent immediately to the 10th Tank Regiment in Tungan, where he was trained as a gunner. He was well educated and understood some English, so he was also trained in radio communication, though he remained assigned as a tank crewman. Along with a number of the more promising young

The 1945 Philippines campaign was the second time the 7th Tank Regiment had fought on Luzon. Here, a Type 89 Chi-Ro Otsu medium tank of the 1st Company, 7th Tank Regiment, crosses an improvised bridge erected to bypass Highway 6 north of Manila on January 3, 1942. The white star was the company insignia. This old tank remained in service in small numbers on Leyte in 1944, serving with the 7th Separate Tank Company. (NARA)

recruits, he was sent back to the Chiba Tank School for a special one-week course in May
1942. He returned to the 10th Tank Regiment and served with it in the Philippines.

Some of the tankers were less experienced. Cpl Y. Suzuki, a 47mm tank gunner of the
2nd Company, 7th Tank Regiment, was conscripted in January 1944, and immediately
sent to the regiment in Manchuria, arriving in February 1944. He received his basic
and advanced training within the regiment and was then sent to the Philippines in
August 1944.

The senior Japanese commanders were all experienced tankers. The commander of
the 2nd Armored Division was Maj Gen Yoshiharu Iwanaka. He commanded the 1st
Tank Regiment in 1937, and was then assigned to the new 7th Tank Regiment in
1938 with the 11th Army in the Wuhan area of central China. Iwanaka was promoted
to major general in 1940 and became the commander of the 1st Tank Group of the
Kwangtung Army, a precursor of the later armored division. He led Japan's premier
tank center, the Chiba Tank School, in 1941–43 and so was influential in establishing
Japanese tank doctrine and training practices. He was promoted to lieutenant general
in 1943 and assigned to command of the 2nd Armored Division on January 8, 1944.
The 3rd Armored Brigade commander was Maj Gen Isao Shigemi. He commanded
the 2nd Separate Tank Company during the Shanghai Incident in 1932 and served
as the commanding officer of the 9th Tank Regiment in 1939–40 before being
assigned as an instructor at the Shihei Tank School in 1940–41. For most of the war
from 1941 through 1944, he was an instructor at the Noncommissioned Officer Tank
School before being appointed to command the 3rd Tank Brigade on March 1, 1944,
prior to its transfer to the Philippines. The commander of the 7th Tank Regiment
was Lt Col Takao Maeda. He had served under Shigemi as a platoon leader during the

Shanghai Incident, and later served in the 5th Tank Regiment during the fighting in China, including the 1939 Nanchang campaign.

One issue affecting the performance of the 7th Tank Regiment on Luzon was medical. While the Japanese soldiers developed a reputation as "jungle supermen" after the stunning victories in 1941 in tropical areas such as Malaya and the Philippines, Japan is not a tropical country, and Japanese soldiers were just as vulnerable as Americans to tropical diseases. Prior to the Philippines deployment, the 7th Tank Regiment was stationed in Manchuria, where the climate is extremely cold in the winter and arid in the summer. While the early winter months in the Philippines are comfortable in terms of temperature, the Japanese troops arriving from Manchuria were hard hit by tropical diseases. Some units of the 2nd Armored Division had as many as a third of their men incapacitated by malaria and dengue fever prior to the January–February 1945 fighting.

JAPANESE TANK ORGANIZATION

The Japanese 7th Tank Regiment was established in central China in 1938 and took part in campaigns there in 1938–39, including the March 1939 Nanchang campaign. In December 1941–May 1942, it participated in the Luzon operations, including the final fighting for Corregidor. After the Philippines campaign, it was stationed at Mutanchiang (Mudanjiang) in southeastern Manchuria and was attached to the 2nd Armored Division when it formed there in June 1942, with the regiment subordinate to the new 3rd Armored Brigade headquarters. The regiment had the cryptonym *Manshu-429* through early 1945; Japanese units never used their actual designations in orders or communications and instead employed cryptonyms like this. It was redesignated as *Geki-12095* in mid January 1945 when the division changed its cryptonyms. When the 2nd Armored Division was ordered to the Philippines in the summer of 1944, the 7th Tank Regiment was transferred to the Korean port of Pusan and began to embark for the Philippines in late August. The regiment was transported aboard the *Amahi Maru* and *Hakusika Maru*, arriving on Luzon in early September 1944. Unlike some of the other units in the division, it suffered few if any losses during the voyage. It was initially deployed at Cabanatuan on the Manila plains, along with the 3rd Armored Brigade headquarters.

Japanese tank regiments in 1944–45 typically had six companies, which included five tank companies and a maintenance company. The regiment had a nominal organization of one light tank company, three medium tank companies, and one "gun tank" company. Two types of "gun tanks" were being developed in Japan in 1944: a turreted assault gun with a 75mm howitzer for fire support, such as the Type 2 Gun Tank Ho-I, and a self-propelled antitank gun in an open casemate such as the Type 1 Ho-Ni. A handful of the new Type 1 Ho-Ni were issued to the 2nd Armored Division, but there were too few for the tank regiments, so they were assigned to a special company attached to the division's artillery regiment and used as a tank-destroyer

Table 4. IJA 7th Tank Regiment organization, January 1945

Unit	Commander	Light tanks	Medium tanks
7th Tank Regiment	Lt Col Takao Maeda	(17)	(54)
HQ section	Capt Masao Amashiro	1	5
1st Company	1st Lt Kunio Nagabuchi	12	0
2nd Company	Capt Sohachi Egi	1	11
3rd Company	Capt Kiyoki Sanemitsu	1	11
4th Company	1st Lt Yoshitaka Takaki	1	11
5th Company	Capt Yoshio Ito	1	11
6th (Maint.) Company	1st Lt Sotaro Hara	0	5

unit. Since there were no actual "gun tanks" available for the gun tank company, the older Type 97 Chi-Ha with the original 57mm gun was used instead, since its 57mm gun offered better HE fire support against unarmored targets than the 47mm gun on the Shinhoto Chi-Ha. At the start of 1945, the 7th Tank Regiment had a total of 801 troops, including 36 officers, 20 warrant officers and 745 enlisted men.

As mentioned earlier, the 7th Tank Regiment was attached to the 2nd Armored Division since its establishment in 1942. In the wake of the Nomonhan defeat, the

Japanese tank regiments in 1945 were supposed to have a single company of gun tanks to provide additional firepower to the weakly armed Type 97-kai. One option was the Type 1 Ho-Ni, which consisted of a Type 97 medium tank chassis with a 75mm Type 90 field gun in an open casemate. Only two of these reached the 2nd Armored Division on Luzon, and they served with the 2nd Mobile Artillery Regiment. This one was captured at Aritao by the 37th Division during the fighting there in early June 1945. (NARA)

IJA planned to create ten armored divisions to serve as a counterweight against Soviet power in the Manchuria area. Following the stunning German victory over France in May–June 1940, the Wehrmacht became the new model for IJA development, and a delegation headed by Gen Tomoyuki Yamashita toured Germany to study the lessons of the recent European fighting. The Yamashita report emphasized the need for mechanization and a switch to medium tanks. Curiously enough, it also warned against any war with the United States, Britain, or the Soviet Union in view of the backward state of IJA equipment. In 1941, the IJA's Kwangtung Army in Manchuria was advocating Japanese participation in the German invasion of the Soviet Union in 1941, which provided added incentive for abundant new armored divisions. Even after this scheme was rejected in favor of the attack on the Philippines, Malaya, and the Dutch East Indies in December 1941, Japan remained wary of Soviet intentions, and the creation of three armored divisions in Manchuria was viewed as a prudent countermeasure. The 1st, 2nd, and 3rd Divisions were organized by the Kwangtung Army in the summer of 1942; the 4th Armored Division was created in Japan in July 1944 for final defense of the Home Islands.

The Japanese armored divisions were fairly typical of *Blitzkrieg*-era armored divisions in Europe and the United States in the 1939–41 period, and they included relatively large tank components but relatively weak infantry and artillery. The division had four tank regiments organized under two tank brigade headquarters, but only one mobile infantry and one mobile artillery regiment. Due to battlefield experiences in 1941–43, the German Army gradually shifted the tank–infantry balance in favor of infantry so that, by 1944, the Panzer divisions had two Panzergrenadier regiments but only a single Panzer regiment. The German Army found that a heavier infantry element was essential in defensive operations of the type that became more common after 1943. American combat experience in Tunisia in early 1943 reaffirmed the need for fewer tanks and more infantry. The US Army armored divisions retained their

The 2nd Mobile Infantry Regiment was motorized rather than mechanized due to the shortage of half-track and tracked personnel carriers. The 2nd Armored Division had at least four of these Hino Motors Type 1 Ho-Ki armored carriers on Luzon. Each could carry up to 24 troops and could also be used as an artillery prime mover. (NARA)

offensive orientation, but shifted the balance from a 6–3–3 mix (six tank, three armored infantry, and three armored artillery battalions) in 1942 to a 3–3–3 mix under the 1943 reorganization.

The only major test of the Japanese armored divisions prior to the Philippines campaign came in the spring of 1944, when the 3rd Armored Division was transferred from the Kwangtung Army to the China Expeditionary Army to take part in the *I-Go* offensive against the Chinese Army. Although the division was used successfully in this operation, it was hardly an adequate test against a modern army.

Regardless of its paper organization, the configuration of the 2nd Armored Division when actually deployed to Luzon in September 1944 was shaped by the declining fortunes of the Kwangtung Army, which was being stripped of its units to assist in the China and Pacific theaters. In January 1944, the 2nd Armored Division lost its 11th Tank Regiment when it was ordered to the Kurile Islands in the north of Japan, facing the Soviet Union. As a result, the remaining three tank regiments (6th, 7th, 10th) were subordinated to 3rd Armored Brigade headquarters and 4th Armored Brigade headquarters became redundant. The division's 2nd Reconnaissance Regiment was detached in February 1944 and reorganized as the 27th Tank Regiment, eventually being deployed to Okinawa. In March 1944 the 2nd Antiaircraft Regiment was taken away and shipped off to China. As a result, the division was significantly shrunken by the time it was ordered to the Philippines in the summer of 1944. Besides these detachments, the division lost additional troops and equipment in the process of transfer to the Philippines, due to the depredations of US Navy submarines and aircraft against the transport convoys. At least six transport ships were sunk; the only major loss of tanks was the 5th Company, 10th Tank Regiment, which lost all of its vehicles, though most of the troops were saved. The division's tank strength was further trimmed after arriving in the Philippines, as the division was pilfered for troops and equipment to reinforce the embattled IJA forces on Leyte, to which two light tank companies were detached.

US TANK CREW

The crew of the M4A3 was five men and their roles were similar to those in the Shinhoto Chi-Ha. The turret crew consisted of the loader in the left side of the turret, the gunner in the front right side of the turret, and the commander behind him on the rear right side, below the main hatch. In the hull, the driver sat on the left side and the co-driver/bow machine-gunner sat on the right. The vehicle radio was carried in the rear turret bustle and was operated by the tank commander, with the assistance of the loader if necessary. In a Sherman platoon of five tanks, the platoon leader was usually a second lieutenant; the platoon sergeant was a staff sergeant; and the remaining commanders "buck" sergeants.

US tank crew training typically included initial basic training, followed by transfer to the tank unit or to specialized training at the Armor School at Fort Knox. In some

cases, tank crew would receive their skills training with their unit, and then be sent to Fort Knox for more advanced training. Most US tank units encouraged cross-training, so that the crew members knew the essentials of all the other positions in the tank.

The 716th Tank Battalion was originally formed in the autumn of 1942 at Camp Chaffee, Arkansas, as the 3rd Battalion, 48th Armored Regiment, 14th Armored Division. The presumption at the time was that the battalion would serve as part of an armored division in the European theater. In the wake of the Tunisia campaign, however, the US Army decided to reorganize the armored divisions, disband the armored regiment headquarters, and reduce the number of tank battalions within

Company D in each US tank battalion was still equipped with the M5A1 light tank. This vehicle was much more comparable in size and weight to the Chi-Ha. Here is an M5A1 named "Ginny" of Company D, 44th Tank Battalion, operating in support of the 1st Cavalry Division on Leyte on October 20, 1944. This battalion later served on Luzon. (NARA)

37

The crew of a US Army M4A1 medium tank, probably from the 762nd Tank Battalion, on Saipan in June 1944. The tanker to the right is looking at the 2in smoke mortar fitted in the upper left corner of the turret in front of the loader. This was a new feature on the Sherman, having been adopted in October 1943. (NARA)

the division from six to three to provide a better balance between tanks, infantry and artillery. On September 20, 1943, 3/48th Armored Regiment was deactivated and the 716th Tank Battalion created in its place. The reorganization of more than a dozen armored divisions created a large pool of separate tank battalions. This restructuring came at an opportune time, as combat experiences in Tunisia, Sicily, and Italy in 1943 had convinced the Headquarters Army Ground Forces (AGF) that there was a persistent need for separate tank battalions to support infantry divisions in combat.[4] Many senior commanders recommended that the new separate tank battalions be immediately assigned to specific infantry divisions for joint training. Unfortunately, the commander of AGF, Lt Gen Lesley McNair, had long opposed incorporation of specialized battalions into the infantry divisions, favoring instead a lean, modular division that could have tank, tank-destroyer, antiaircraft, and other specialized battalions added in-theater as the occasion warranted. In the end, this position would prove misguided, as the most vital lesson learned in both the European and Pacific theaters was that joint tank–infantry training was essential and was best accomplished if the tank battalion was organic to the infantry division.

US tank battalions under the new 1943 TO&E consisted of a headquarters company, service company and four tank companies, lettered A through D. Companies A, B, and C were equipped with medium tanks, while Company D was equipped with M5A1 light tanks. Each medium tank company had an HQ and three platoons. The HQ had two medium tanks and one M4 (105mm) assault gun, while the three

---

4. See Steven J. Zaloga, *US Armored Units in the North African and Italian Campaigns 1942–45*, Battle Orders 21, Osprey, Oxford (2006)

platoons each had five M4A3 medium tanks. The battalion HQ had a command tank for the battalion commander and executive officer, and an assault-gun platoon with three more M4 (105mm) assault guns. This structure meant the 716th Tank Battalion had 53 M4A3 medium tanks, 6 M4 (105mm) assault guns, 17 M5A1 light tanks, and 748 men, making it almost identical in size to the Japanese 7th Tank Regiment.

The new 716th Tank Battalion was dispatched to Louisiana in late November 1943 to participate in the Fifth Phase 3rd Army maneuvers, a vast eight-week wargame conducted in the cold rain, mud, and snow of severe winter weather. The battalion then departed for Camp Howze, Texas, where the post-maneuver training focused on tank-crew gunnery and unit combat tests under the supervision of the 12th Armored Division. In April 1944, the battalion was earmarked as one of the reinforcements being sent to MacArthur in the Southwest Pacific Area (SWPA) for the campaigns in the Philippines expected later in 1944. The battalion departed from the West Coast on May 21, 1944, for a 27-day voyage to Buna, New Guinea. The troops constructed their own base camp until their equipment arrived on later transports, and then they began limited training with the 38th Division. Extensive tank–infantry training was seldom possible, as the jungle base camps simply didn't have the maneuver room. Prior to the Luzon campaign, Company A was sent to join the 6th Division at Sansapor, Company C to Aitape to join the 43rd Division, and Companies B and D along with the rest of the HQ and service companies to join other elements of the 43rd Division on Hollandia. All these scattered units embarked for Luzon in December 1944. The battalion conducted an assault landing as part of I Corps on White Beach 2 and Blue Beach on the Lingayen Gulf of Luzon on January 9, 1945, at the start of Operation *Mike-1*.

As fate would have it, Company C, 716th Tank Battalion, was not assigned to the 43rd Division with which it had trained, but was assigned to 25th "Tropic Lightning" Division. During the battle for San Manuel, it was attached to the division's 161st Infantry Regiment. The 161st Infantry was a veteran unit of the SWPA campaigns, having seen combat on Guadalcanal starting in December 1942, the Munda airfield battles, and the New Georgia campaign in the northern Solomons in the spring and summer of 1943. The regiment was withdrawn from combat in early November 1943 after nearly a year of combat and refitted and trained on Guadalcanal, New Zealand, and New Caledonia prior to the Luzon campaign. These earlier campaigns were in tropical jungles and the regiment was not accustomed to operating with tank support. Indeed, the separate Army tank battalions did not begin to see extensive combat in the SWPA campaigns until 1944, and the vast distances and disparate terrain and conditions did not foster much sharing of "lessons learned." Some veteran SWPA tank battalions, such as the 754th Tank Battalion, did see combat again on Luzon.

Both the Japanese 7th Tank Regiment and the American 716th Tank Battalion were well-trained and well-equipped by their own national standards when committed to the Luzon campaign in January 1945, but neither had any recent combat experience. Both units had been created to fight in very different conditions. They were inexperienced in combat, and were employed by higher commands lacking any real experience in the use of tank units, since tank combat in the Pacific theater had been sporadic and on a small scale until the summer of 1944. As a result, the combat performance of both units depended on the ability of local commands to adapt quickly to the circumstances.

THE STRATEGIC SITUATION

The summer campaigns of 1944 were critical steps towards the looming defeat of Japan. The amphibious assaults in the Marianas at Saipan, Guam, and Tinian in June–August 1944 put the US Army Air Force's B-29 Superfortress bombers within range of the Japanese Home Islands. The defeat of the Japanese navy in the battle of the Philippine Sea marked the death knell of Japanese carrier aviation, and the battle is better known as the "Marianas Turkey Shoot" in US Navy history due to the unequal nature of the air battles. To amplify Japan's predicament, MacArthur's forces in the SWPA had "leap-frogged" up from New Guinea in the summer of 1944 with a series of small but vital landings on islands on the southern approaches to the Philippines.

Although Japan's Imperial General Headquarters (IGHQ) considered it possible that the United States would launch attacks towards Japan's inner defense belt directly from the Marianas, the presumption was that the Philippines would be invaded as a pre-requisite for the final campaign against Japan. The IGHQ planning in the late summer of 1944 expected a US assault on the Palau islands followed by a Philippines operation in November 1944. As expected, the US Marines landed on Peleliu in the Palaus in September 1944. The Philippines were absolutely vital to Japan, since American liberation of the islands would put the United States in immediate striking range of the main shipping routes from Malaya and the Dutch East Indies, which provided Japan with essential raw materials and fuel oil. The advance would be a further stepping stone towards Japan from the south.

Until the summer of 1944, the Philippines had been used mainly as a training base and staging area for Japanese forces on the outer defensive belt. In May 1944, the 14th Area Army in the Philippines had only a single division and four brigades, with

Questions about the validity of the IJA's "Waterline Defense" doctrine came into sharp focus following the Japanese defeat on Saipan in June–July 1944. Conforming to the standard tactic, the 9th Tank Regiment staged a counterattack against the beach-head on the night of June 15–16, and was wiped out. Here, three Marines survey the battlefield the following morning, standing in front of a Type 95 tank with its turret blown off and a Type 97 in the background. (NARA)

a second division in the process of transfer. The defense of the Philippines was a daunting task, in view of the enormous geographic extent of the islands and the lack of any firm intelligence on where the Americans were likely to attack. There was a general consensus that the main objective was the island of Luzon, due to the presence of the capital Manila there as well as the pre-war Clark Field airbase. However, there was also some expectation in Tokyo that the US forces would seize one of the other islands first as a prelude to the main assault on Luzon, perhaps Mindanao. Uncertainty over the likely site of the initial American invasion forced the IJA to scatter its forces over several of the main islands. Reinforcements came from Manchuria, Formosa (Taiwan), and Korea.

The string of American victories in the Central Pacific in 1943–44 raised serious doubts about the IJA's doctrine for island defense. Japanese tactical doctrine through mid 1944 was based on "waterline defense," a vigorous defense along the beach using fortifications followed by a violent counter-offensive against the beach-head using mobile forces, including any available tank units. This tactic continued to fail, most clearly on Saipan in June 1944 when the counterattack against the beachhead by the 9th Tank Regiment had been snuffed out with catastrophic losses to the attacker and negligible losses to the defending US Marine units. Likewise, when the tank company of the 14th Division on Peleliu counterattacked the Marine beach-head, it was wiped out.

In mid August 1944, the IGHQ released the first major new Japanese tactical manual since 1928, the "Essentials of Island Defense." This manual marked a growing shift away from committing the bulk of the defense close to the beach due to its vulnerability to US naval gunfire, and instead recommended a protracted defense based on layered fortified lines. The theory was further amended in October 1944 with a draft of a new counter-amphibious doctrine, which completely rejected water's edge defense in favor of inland defense-in-depth. This policy was extremely controversial, and in the event it arrived barely in time to influence the opening phase of the Philippines campaign in October 1944.

On October 17, 1944, US forces began landings on the small islands in Leyte Gulf, followed by the main landings by Gen Walter Krueger's 6th Army on Leyte itself on October 20, 1944. As the IGHQ had surmised, these landings were only preliminary operations in support of an eventual attack on Luzon. There was a substantial debate within Tokyo whether or not to reinforce the 16th Division on Leyte, or to withhold forces for the eventual battle on Luzon. In the event, Leyte was reinforced at the expense of Luzon, with five IJA divisions being destroyed in the fighting from late October to the end of December 1944, thereby substantially weakening any possible defense of Luzon. The fighting for Leyte also saw the last stand of the IJN, with its crushing defeat in the battle of Leyte Gulf in late October.

The expenditure of so many troops in the futile defense of Leyte greatly limited the tactical options available to Gen Tomoyuki Yamashita, commander of the 14th Area Army on Luzon. There was no expectation that this badly depleted force could successfully resist an initial American amphibious landing. As a result, the defense planners rejected the idea of waging a decisive battle intended to defeat the US Army on Luzon, in favour of the more limited objective of delaying the American conquest of Luzon and inflicting the maximum number of casualties. The most obvious political objective on Luzon was the capital Manila, but Yamashita rejected plans to focus the 14th Area Army on the defense of the city. Instead, Yamashita decided to focus on withdrawing the main elements of the 14th Area Army into three mountainous bastions, where his limited forces could conduct a prolonged defense. Yamashita would command the largest of these concentrations, the Shobu Group, in the Cordillera Central and Sierra Madre mountains of northern Luzon. Defense in this mountain fastness would stymie subsequent US attacks towards Formosa or Okinawa, and the terrain was well suited to a campaign of prolonged attrition. Although there was no certainty where the US forces were likely to land, there was a strong expectation that it would be at Lingayen Gulf on the west-central coast of Luzon, where the Japanese Army itself had landed in 1941.

MacArthur indeed selected the Lingayen Gulf for precisely the same reasons as the IJA had done in 1941, though MacArthur chose a location slightly to the west of the Japanese landing site. The Lingayen Gulf offered excellent landing beaches, with open terrain behind to provide a deep beach-head suited to building up forces for subsequent operations. It was the northern end of the Central Plains corridor leading to Clark Field and Manila. The only other plausible landing site was in the Manila Bay area, but this area was more congested and was plagued by numerous terrain bottlenecks.

A combat manual issued by the 2nd Armored Division on November 15, 1944, opened with the admonition that "This Philippines battle will end either in the annihilation of the American devils or in the complete destruction of our forces. The decisive day is drawing near… Emphasis must be placed on antitank combat, especially against their heavy tanks. Our lack of armament is more than equaled by our divine ability and superior tactics."

The planned role for the 2nd Armored Division changed repeatedly in the weeks before the US landings. Although Yamashita had skillfully used tank regiments in

the 1941–42 campaign in Malaya, he was not especially confident of the value of an armored division in the Philippines. A 2nd Armored Division officer later recalled that:

> Gen Yamashita, being an old-time infantry soldier, did not believe in mechanized warfare. When the 2nd Armored Division landed in Manila, Gen Yamashita expressed great displeasure and was unenthusiastic about the unit from the outset. There were no tank specialists attached to Gen Yamashita's headquarters. So after the division landed, it was split up. The division commander's pleas to keep it together were not backed by anybody in the headquarters. Yamashita thought that if the division was split up it could attack US troops wherever they landed on Luzon. One unit could immediately engage them and could then be reinforced by the division's other units. If it was concentrated in one area, Yamashita was afraid that it would be annihilated by air attacks. The dispersed units served as a counterweight against US airborne landings. The continual shifting of the units from place to place wore down the equipment and troops, and their consumption of rations and fuel convinced the general that they were more trouble than they were worth.

Under the mid December 1944 plans, the bulk of the 2nd Armored Division was stationed in the Cabanatuan area on the Central Plains, centrally located between the landings sites on the Lingayen Gulf and Manila, and near to Clark Field. Yamashita was concerned that the Americans might launch a paratroop landing on the Central Plains or against Clark Field, and the 2nd Armored Division would provide a mobile response against such lightly armed forces. The division was assigned control of the Kembu Group, which consisted of the armored division along with nearly 30,000 assorted troops drawn from both combat and administrative units. The mission of the Kembu Group was to hold Clark Field and to threaten any American advance down the Manila plains. Once the Clark Field defenses were overcome, the Kembu Group was to withdraw into the Zambales mountains to the west of the air base and conduct a protracted battle of attrition. Towards the end of December, a battlegroup created from the division's main infantry element, the 2nd Mobile Infantry Regiment, was the first element of the division to be deployed at Clark Field. Another battlegroup based on the 6th Tank Regiment was detached from the division and directed to the Manila area.

During the first week of January 1945, Japanese reconnaissance picked up strong evidence of US naval forces moving towards the Lingayen Gulf, and on January 6, US warships began a preliminary bombardment of the beach area. Yamashita ordered the 2nd Armored Division to form a battlegroup to reinforce the 23rd Division, which was holding the eastern shoulder of the Lingayen Gulf area. This was an especially vital assignment, as not only did this sector adjoin the Lingayen Gulf, but it controlled the access routes into the mountainous bastion in northern Luzon. Due to the importance of this mission, the battlegroup was formed from the headquarters elements of the 3rd Armored Brigade under Gen Shigemi and consisted of the bulk of the 7th Tank Regiment, reinforced with the last remaining infantry battalion of the 2nd Mobile Infantry Regiment and a field artillery battalion. It immediately began moving towards Urdaneta.

On January 8, the remaining elements of the 2nd Armored Division still in the Cabanatuan area were ordered to reinforce the Clark Field defenses. In the event, this movement was cut short the next day when US forces began landing on the Lingayen Gulf. The mission of the 2nd Armored Division now completely changed and its uncommitted forces were ordered instead to move northwest to Tayug along the Agno River. Its new mission was to create a potential counterattack force to strike the left flank of any American attack down the Central Plains to Manila. By this stage, the division was broken up into three main chunks. The Takayama Group, formed from the 2nd Mobile Infantry Regiment, remained committed to the defense of Clark Field. The Shigemi Group was the vanguard of the division and moving towards Lingayen Gulf. The majority of the division, including both the Ida Group (6th Tank Regiment) and Harada Group (10th Tank Regiment), was moving towards the Agno River line.

US Army planners were well aware of the presence of the armored division on Luzon, but were uncertain about its mission or its likely scheme of action. There was concern about its potential use as a massed mobile force, but there was also some evidence from intelligence coming from China and Manchuria that the Japanese armored divisions tended to be used in a disjointed and dispersed fashion. Due to the potential threat of the 2nd Armored Division, the *Mike-1* plans for the Luzon landings envisioned a more elaborate use of armor than in previous campaigns in the Southwest Pacific. Each of the two corps taking part in the initial landings was assigned a single tank battalion for support, the inexperienced 716th Tank Battalion with I Corps on the left flank, and the veteran 754th Tank Battalion with the XIV Corps on the right flank. To provide a potential counterweight to the Japanese 2nd Armored Division, the 13th Armored Group was assigned to the 6th Army.

Company B, 716th Tank Battalion, sets up defensive positions in the bluffs over the landing beaches on January 9 following the initial Luzon landings by I Corps on the left flank of the Sixth Army attack. The M4A3 tank still has its wading trunks fitted. (NARA)

Armored groups are the least familiar type of US Army tank formation during the war. They had been created in 1942 as a means to control the separate tank battalions not assigned to armored divisions. The original scheme was to use them as tactical commands that could form the kernel of small armored battlegroups with two or more tank battalions. In the event, the US Army saw a greater need to provide infantry divisions with tank support, and so the practice in both Europe and the Pacific was to disperse the tank battalions to infantry divisions rather than keep them concentrated under the armored groups. The armored groups remained in existence, but in most cases they became administrative units used to provide technical support to dispersed tank battalions rather than to serve in their original role as tactical headquarters. The use of the 13th Armored Group on Luzon was a rare case of applying them as a tactical headquarters of an armored battlegroup. The 13th Armored Group included the 44th and 775th Tank Battalions, the 632nd Tank-Destroyer Battalion, and the 156th Engineer Combat Battalion, and it landed in the I Corps sector of Lingayen Gulf on January 11. In the event, the Japanese 2nd Armored Division was not used as a mobile counterattack force, and so the various elements of the 13th Armored Group were gradually doled out for the traditional infantry support mission and it was not used as a concentrated armored force.

COMBAT

On January 9 the 716th Tank Battalion landed on White Beach in support of the 43rd Division. The battalion was immediately dispersed to support the 43rd Division on a scale of one company per infantry regiment. For the first week of fighting, the scattered companies were committed to the standard infantry support role, most notably in the attacks in the Cabaruan Hills on the southeastern side of the "Beachhead Line." The commander of the 716th Tank Battalion, Lt Col Lorwyn Peterson, was killed in action on January 19, 1945, while trying to rescue a crewman from a disabled assault gun; for his actions he was posthumously awarded the Silver Star. Company C, commanded by Capt John Huntington, remained in reserve until January 17 when it was sent towards Binalonan.

The Shigemi Group was subordinated to the 23rd Division to assist in counterattacks against the American beachhead. Capt Sohachi Egi's 2nd Light Tank Company was detached from the 7th Tank Regiment, placed directly under 23rd Division command, and sent to the Cabu area for anti-paratroop patrol; as a result it was the one element of the regiment that would not be destroyed at San Manuel. On January 10, Lt Gen Fukutaro Nishiyama, 23rd Division commander, ordered the Shigemi Group to mass in the San Manuel area, and on January 12 he directed the group to move forward to Binalonan and Urdaneta to destroy US tank units operating in the Cabaruan hills area in support of US infantry divisions. The 7th Tank Regiment began moving forces towards Urdaneta to attack the elements of the 716th Tank Battalion moving forward from Manaoag. Since much of Shigemi's group was strung out on the road, the 3rd and 4th Companies, 7th Tank Regiment, deployed detachments to these two key towns until the rest of the scattered units arrived. On January 14, the 23rd Division ordered a simultaneous counterattack of the American beach-head in the pre-dawn hours of January 17 by four "suicide penetration units" (*Kesshi Teishin Kirikomi-tai*), three of these

Here is one of three M4A3s of Lt Robert Courtwright's platoon, Company A, 716th Tank Battalion, that was knocked out in an ambush by Type 97-kai Shinhoto Chi-Ha tanks of Warrant Officer Kojura Wada's platoon from the 3rd Company, 7th Tank Regiment, during the fighting for Urdaneta on January 17, 1945. (NARA)

from the infantry regiments, and a fourth drawn from the Shigemi Group. In the event, this major counterattack against the Lingayen Gulf beach-head degenerated into a series of disjointed and ineffective attacks.

The raiding element of the Shigemi Group was the 4th Company, 7th Tank Regiment led by 1st Lt Yoshitaka Takaki, supported by a company of infantry from the 1st Battalion, 2nd Mobile Infantry Regiment, which had deployed to Binalonan. The Takaki Detachment was supposed to strike from Manaoag, but on the night of January 15–16 its spearhead patrol of three tanks unexpectedly ran into elements of the US Army's 103rd Infantry, 43rd Division, in the village of Malasin, an event that made it clear that Manaoag was already in American hands. The Takaki Detachment launched an attack shortly before midnight on January 16–17 against 3/103rd Infantry in the village of Potpot. A few M4A3 tanks of Company C, 716th Tank Battalion, had reached the 103rd Infantry by this time. In the darkness, the Japanese tanks bumped into the American defense perimeter and two tanks passed through the infantry battalion and continued down the road towards Manaoag. The final tank in the column was knocked out. After a short delay, the main body of the Takaki Detachment struck the American perimeter, starting a confused two-hour skirmish in the dark. By the end of the fight, 3/103rd Infantry had lost two men killed and ten wounded as well as an M8 armored car, a jeep and a 37mm gun destroyed; in addition, a jeep, an M8 armored car, and an M4A3 were damaged. The Takaki Detachment lost three medium tanks and one light tank and about 50 troops; four other tanks were disabled. The next day, a Japanese soldier recorded in his diary: "It's pitiful. The raid failed. The commanders of the Takaki

Tank Detachment, 2nd Infantry Company, two tank platoon commanders, and one infantry platoon leader were all killed. Six tanks were destroyed and the two infantry companies lost half their troops."

On January 17, the US 103rd Infantry was replaced by the 161st Infantry from the 25th Division and the attack continued up the road into Binalonan itself, where the remnants of the Takaki Detachment along with reinforcements from the 3rd and 5th Tank Companies had set up defensive positions. At 1730hrs, a single Type 97-kai emerged from the town and began firing at the US infantry. It was knocked out, but was quickly followed by a disorganized counterattack by five more tanks which were also destroyed by the 161st Infantry. The following day, the 161st Infantry, supported by Company C, 716th Tank Battalion, cleared Binalonan; in the fight for the town, the 7th Tank Regiment lost nine tanks, two 75mm field guns and about 250 troops. Two tank company commanders – Capt Kiyoki Sanemitsu (3rd Company) and Capt Yoshio Ito (5th Company) – were killed in the fighting. The remnants of the forward detachments retreated to San Manuel in the pre-dawn darkness of January 19.

To the south, Company A, 716th Tank Battalion, was taken from battalion reserves and sent to assist 3/1st Infantry, 6th Infantry Division during an attack on Urdaneta on the morning of January 17. This town was garrisoned by other tank platoons from the 3rd Company, 7th Tank Regiment, and a company of infantry. As 3/1st Infantry advanced towards the town, the lead rifle platoons were forced to ground by Japanese mortar and machine-gun fire. A platoon of M4A3 tanks led by Lt Robert Courtwright moved towards the town, but had difficulty engaging the Japanese positions on their left flank due to the presence of friendly infantry. It was a dangerous predicament, as hidden in a mango grove were Warrant Officer Kojura Wada's platoon of three Type 97-kai tanks. Wada warned his crews to wait until the American tanks were close and only to engage them against their thinner side armor. At a range of only about 35 yards,

A platoon of tanks from the 716th Tank Battalion supports the 158th Infantry, attached to the 43rd Division, during the fighting along the Damortis–Rosario road on January 17, 1945. (NARA)

49

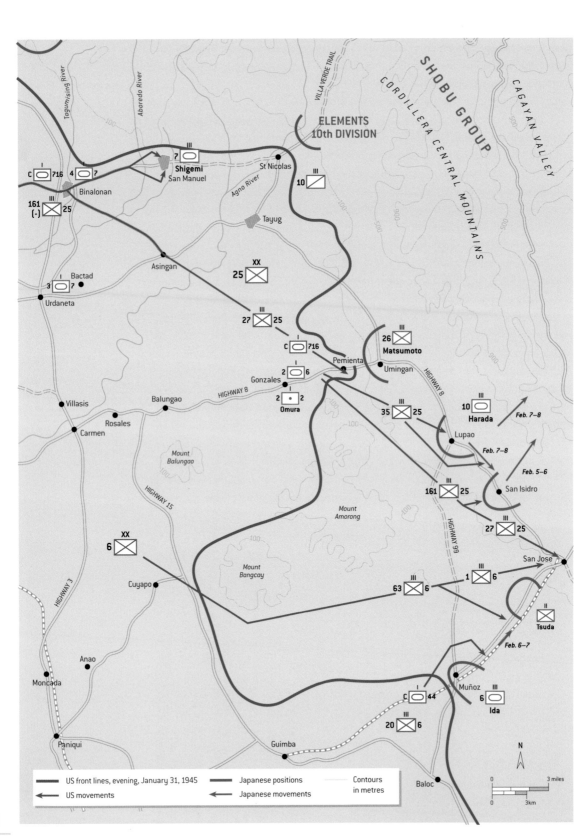

SHOBU GROUP

CORDILLERA CENTRAL MOUNTAINS

CAGAYAN VALLEY

VILLA VERDE TRAIL

ELEMENTS
10th DIVISION

Tagumising River

Aboredo River

Agno River

C | 716
4 | 7

III
7

Shigemi
San Manuel

St Nicolas

III
10

Binalonan

161 [-] III 25

Bactad

3 | 7

Urdaneta

Asingan

XX
25

Tayug

27 III 25

C | 716

III
26
Matsumoto

Umingan

HIGHWAY 8

Pemienta

Gonzales

2 | 6

2 • 2
Omura

35 III 25

III
10
Harada

Feb. 7–8

Lupao

Feb. 7–8

Feb. 5–6

161 III 25

San Isidro

27 III 25

Villasis

Balungao

HIGHWAY 8

Rosales

Carmen

Mount
Balungao

HIGHWAY 15

Mount
Amorong

HIGHWAY 99

XX
6

Mount
Bangcay

Cuyapo

63 III 6

1 III 6

San Jose

II
Tsuda

Feb. 6–7

HIGHWAY 3

Anao

Moncada

C | 44

Muñoz

6 III **Ida**

20 III 6

Paniqui

Guimba

N

Baloc

| ▬▬▬ US front lines, evening, January 31, 1945 | ▬▬▬ Japanese positions | Contours in metres |
| ◄─── US movements | ◄─── Japanese movements | |

0   3 miles
0   3km

50

Wada's tanks began firing in quick succession, disabling two of the M4A3 tanks immediately, including Courtwright's, and then knocking the track off Sgt Shrift's tank.

Shrift's driver was able to use the undamaged track to swing the M4A3 towards Wada's three tanks, shielding the tank with the thicker front armor. Shrift's crew quickly engaged the Japanese tanks, and Wada's was the first tank knocked out, by hits to the engine and hull. The Japanese tanks continued to fire, and expended about 60 rounds in the engagement, with many of the rounds bouncing off the thick frontal armor of Shrift's M4A3. The second Japanese tank, commanded by Sgt Kokai, received a hit through the gun mantlet, so Wada ordered Sgt Suzuki's surviving tank to attack Shrift's M4A3 at close range. Suzuki managed to maneuver closer and hit Shrift's tank, but his own tank was destroyed by direct hits from Shrift's 75mm gun.

Company A's losses included the total loss of one tank and two disabled, along with two tankers killed and two wounded. Wada's platoon lost all three tanks. Shrift and his crew were awarded the Silver Star for their actions. The attack into Urdaneta continued and the town was eventually taken. The Japanese detachment lost nine tanks and about 100 troops, while 3/1st Infantry suffered five killed and 15 wounded. In total, the fighting in the I Corps sector on January 16–17 cost the advance guards of the Shigemi Group a total of 19 Type 97 medium tanks and three Type 95 light tanks.

PLANS RECONSIDERED

Gen Yamashita was forced to reconsider his deployments in mid January due to the speedy American advance out of the Lingayen Gulf beach-head. His most pressing problem was the vulnerability of the town of San Jose, the major access route into the Cagayen Valley and the mountains of northern Luzon, where the Shobu Group was intended to set up its final defense. Yamashita had ordered the 10th Division to shield this sector, but for a variety of reasons his orders had been ignored. Yamashita's only recourse was to redirect the 2nd Armored Division from its recently assigned defense sector north of St Nicolas behind the Shigemi Group, to move instead to the towns in the foreground of San Jose, notably Muñoz and Lupao. Another reason for this change in deployment was the sudden recognition that the Villa Verde trail into the mountains behind St Nicolas was not adequate for heavy vehicular traffic, and if the bulk of the division had been deployed there as originally planned, it would have been trapped.

As mentioned earlier, the Shigemi Group could not carry out its intended deployment to Binalonan, so it was ordered to hold the town of San Manuel to shield the rest of the 2nd Armored Division while they deployed in front of San Jose. On January 20, Gen Shigemi issued orders to his forces in San Manuel: "The group will defend its present position to the death. The enemy must be annihilated and we will hold San Manuel at all costs."

The tactical approach for the forthcoming battle was to use the tanks as semi-mobile pillboxes, operating from hull-down entrenchments. The towns were ringed with tank

OPPOSITE
Destruction of the Japanese 2nd Armored Division, January 1945.

revetments, and inner layers of revetments were dug through the town to allow the tanks to cover major roads, streets, and intersections. Many of the tank revetments had an accompanying set of rifle pits and machine-gun emplacements for close defense. All of the revetments were well camouflaged – the defenses took advantage of the extensive vegetation at the edges of the town. There were also large clumps of bamboo here, with the thickets sometimes being 20–30ft in diameter. There were also a number of revetments for the towed artillery and antitank guns.

San Manuel had a total of about 75 tank revetments, which were close in number to the full strength of a tank regiment. As described earlier, the Shigemi Group had suffered numerous tank losses in the earlier fighting, and so by the time of the battle for San Manuel, the group had been reduced to only about 50 tanks. Some of the tanks were assigned in a semi-permanent fashion to the outer defense perimeter. Even in these cases, most tanks had alternative revetments, so that in the event that a position came under particularly intense fire, the tank could reverse out of the revetment and move to a safer position. Besides the tanks posted to the perimeter, Shigemi kept a mobile reserve near the center of the town. This permitted the dispatch of tanks to any sector that was threatened. The artillery element of the Shigemi Group included six 105mm howitzers with their prime movers, seven Type 90 75mm field

A column of tanks from Company C, 716th Tank Battalion, with troops of the 103rd Infantry aboard, moves forward through Manaoag on January 15, 1945 during the advance towards Binalonan and San Manuel. (NARA)

guns, two 47mm antitank guns, and nine 50mm mortars. On first contact, the US Army thought that there were only about 600 troops in the town, but the actual figure was almost double. Many of the troops were from divisional service units who were deployed as riflemen in the "spider hole" defenses near the tanks, or who were assigned to the many "suicide raiding groups" dispatched from the town during the course of the fighting.

The decision to entrench the division's tanks was controversial, and the source of considerable criticism after the fighting. Col Shigeo Kawaii, the division's operations officer, later explained the rationale for the tactic:

> The employment of the tank division in the Philippines is generally considered a great blunder. The fact remains that the Americans had command of the air, preventing movement along the highways and cross-country movement in an area covered with rice paddies was impossible. Consequently, even though the tanks were organized for maneuver combat, they were soon immobilized because of a lack of air cover and the destructive American air attacks which the tanks could not counter. They were, therefore, converted into armored, fixed defenses to be used by the infantry in key positions along defense lines. This adaptation of the tanks was so successful that, in one instance, a line 60 kilometers long was held for a period of one month.

Kawaii's rationale is somewhat disingenuous. None of the defensive positions withstood American infantry attacks for more than a few days. The threat of American

This is a Type 97-kai Shinhoto Chi-Ha of the 3rd Company, 7th Tank Regiment, knocked out during the Binalonan fighting. The markings on the hull side include the *oka* (cherry blossom) marking of the 3rd Company, while in front of it is the traditional *tomoe* design, derived from the family crest of Oishi Kuranosuke, leader of the legendary 47 *ronin* warriors of 1702. On the side of the gun cover is an *ai-koku* presentation marking consisting of two stylized circular characters above, No. 125 in the center, and the symbols for *Dai Nippon* (Greater Japan) below. (NARA)

air attack was a significant concern for Japanese commanders, since they lacked their usual antiaircraft regiment, but one that had little impact on the actual progress of the campaign. The decision to expend the division in a static role was partly due to the last-minute decisions forced on Yamashita by the tactical circumstances because the division was the only one able to set up a defense perimeter in time to shield San Jose and access into the Shobu Group's northern mountain bastion. The 14th Area Army had long hoped to use the 2nd Armored Division as a mobile counterattack force against the US Army on the Manila plains, but this option disappeared due to the unexpectedly rapid US Army advance out of the beach-head line. In addition, the rough handling of the tank companies from the Shigemi Group at Binalonan and Urdaneta simply reinforced the doubts of many senior Japanese commanders about

47MM TYPE 1 TELESCOPE

The Japanese Type 1 gun sight was a 4-power sight. This strength was more than adequate in the Luzon fighting, since combat usually occurred at point-blank ranges. The sight reticle included a set of conventional steps below the cross-hairs to permit the gunner to elevate the gun to compensate for range. The reticle markings were at 300m (328-yard) intervals with the maximum range at 2,000m (2,187 yards). There was no distinction between APHE and HE ammunition. The range data was provided to the gunner by the tank commander based on a ranging reticle in his periscopic sight, though at point-blank ranges as on Luzon, the ranging information was not really necessary.

the division's ability to conduct mobile defensive operations, due to the thin armor of the Japanese tanks and the overwhelming firepower available to American ground forces. Fortifying the tanks held out the hope of prolonging the battles of attrition against US forces.

Shigemi's most significant tactical dilemma was finding a source of infantry to amplify the tank defenses. Even with so many tanks concentrated in a small town, the tanks could be isolated and individually eliminated by a US infantry force unless protected by Japanese infantry. The Shigemi Group originally had an infantry

M71D TELESCOPE

This illustration shows the view through the gunner's M71D telescope. A typical set of commands by the commander to the gunner were: "Gunner – Shot (armor-piercing) – Traverse right – Steady – On – Tank (target) – Two hundred (range of 200 yards) – Fire!" As will be noticed, the commander gave the gunner the range to target based on observation through his binoculars or via his periscopic sight, both of which included ranging reticles. The reticle was selected depending on the ammunition in use, and the ammunition type can be seen at the top. The range lines are in hundreds of yards in 200-yard increments going to 4,200 yards. The deflection lead lines, the horizontal lines on either side of the vertical axes, are spaced 5 mils apart, a mil representing one yard at 1,000 yards' distance. These deflection-lead lines were used by the gunner to determine the amount of lead to give to a moving target; on Luzon this was seldom necessary.

battalion for this role, but two of its three companies had been badly beaten up in the previous week of fighting around Binalonan and Urdaneta. Yamashita was not especially interested in armored division organization and tactics, and showed little awareness of this issue. While he might have reinforced the armored group defenses with infantry companies from neighboring infantry divisions, this was done only in the case of the Ida Group at Muñoz.

THE REDUCTION OF SAN MANUEL

San Manuel was in the sector assigned to Maj Gen Charles Mullins' 25th Division. On January 19, I Corps assigned the division to secure crossings over the Agno River and to begin to reconnoiter eastward 10 miles beyond, prior to moving eastward. Although the divisional frontage of some 30 miles was far in excess of usual US Army tactical doctrine, I Corps had reasonably good intelligence on Japanese divisions and appreciated that Japanese defenses in this sector, aside from San Manuel, were quite sparse. In addition to the traditional means of intelligence gathering, I Corps also had the benefit of a very active Filipino guerilla force, which kept track of Japanese troop deployments in the entire area and reported them to US forces. The capture of San Manuel was assigned to the 161st RCT commanded by Col James Dalton. It consisted of two of the 161st Infantry's three battalions (1st and 2nd), supported by Company C, 716th Tank Battalion, plus one platoon of M5A1 light tanks of Company D, 716th Tank Battalion, and the 98th Chemical Mortar Battalion equipped with 4.2in mortars. The 161st RCT was supported by several field artillery battalions for much of the operation. Although Dalton expected a stiff fight at San Manuel, there was no knowledge of Shigemi's "stand to the death" orders and there was the expectation that after a stiff fight like that at Binalonan and Urdaneta, the Japanese garrison would withdraw into the neighboring mountains to fight another day.

On January 19, following the capture of Binalonan, the 1st Platoon, Company D, 716th Tank Battalion, led by Lt John Griffin, was sent on a patrol to scout out the Japanese defenses around San Manuel. They were supported by a patrol of M4A3 medium tanks from Company C. Shigemi had adamantly insisted that his tank and gun crews maintain strict fire discipline, and that enemy troops only be engaged at close range. As a result, when the M5A1 light tank platoon approached San Manuel, it reached the western outskirts of town before coming under an intense volley of fire. Two M5A1 light tanks were destroyed, with seven crewmen killed and one wounded during the brief skirmish. The remaining tanks withdrew under covering fire from the M4A3 medium tanks. Some M4A3 tanks of Company C remained on the outskirts of San Manuel over the next several days, occasionally firing at targets of opportunity at the western edge of the town, as well as directing artillery fire.

Infantry patrols supported by Filipino guerillas now began probing the San Manuel defenses, starting on January 19. To Col Dalton's surprise, the Shigemi Group had not deployed any significant forces on the north side of San Manuel, most notably on the spur ridge about a mile north of the town. This ridge rose to about 850ft, and so offered an excellent vantage point. American patrols overwhelmed a weak platoon of Japanese infantry in a small outpost on the ridge, and another detachment in a village at the foot of the ridge in order to permit the 161st RCT to deploy 2/161st Infantry in this area prior to the attack. Dalton's plan was to attack the town from two directions: the main blow from 2/161st Infantry against the northern section of the town, and a secondary blow against the southwest corner of the town along the Binalonan road by 1/161st Infantry supported by Company C, 716th Tank Battalion.

The attack started against the southwest corner of town at 0700hrs on January 24, opening with a 15-minute preparatory barrage by the divisional artillery. A Japanese tanker recalled in his diary:

Around dawn, we received the order for all personnel to take their battle positions. I immediately jumped into the tank. The enemy artillery shelling became terrific. When the artillery finally ceased firing, I could distinctly notice the enemy automatic rifle fire sounding like roasting beans, and the sound of our heavy machine guns could be heard intermingled with the enemy's. Can the sound of the automatic cannon fire be the sign of the approach of the M4 tanks? At this moment, our 10cm gun began banging away. For about an hour, its noise mingled with small-arms fire and my confidence was great. In the meantime, Matsui came rushing up. Two M4 tanks had been destroyed and one was on fire. The enemy infantry is withdrawing…

The attack by 1/161st Infantry was preceded by the Company C M4A3 tanks, which reached to within 300 yards of the southwestern corner of town before the US artillery barrage lifted. The Japanese defenses here were among the densest of any

Lt Kunio Nagabuchi's 1st Tank Company, 7th Tank Regiment, was equipped with the Type 95 light tank, and one of these tanks is seen destroyed in front of a house in San Manuel after the fighting. (NARA)

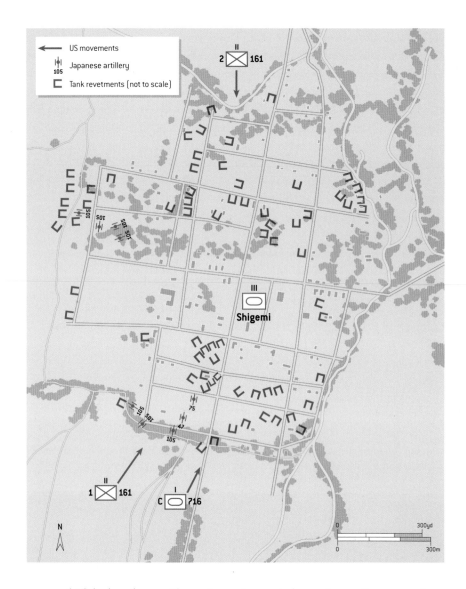

sector, which had not been evident prior to the attack due to the excellent camouflage. Japanese fire discipline was strict, and the M4A3 tanks were not engaged until they were at point-blank range of about 150 yards. At this point, the tanks were suddenly raked by cannon and machine-gun fire, the firepower including tank guns, a 47mm antitank gun, and two 105mm howitzers. Several tanks were hit in the original volley and came to a halt. The tank advance was stopped not only by the Japanese fire, but also by a drainage ditch. One tank attempted to leap the ditch on the run, but instead became stuck in the opposite bank. The infantry deployed near the tanks and began to fire against the Japanese positions, but to little avail. The tanks engaged the Japanese positions and, according to Japanese records, at least two Japanese tanks were knocked out. Cpl Mizoguchi, commanding a Type 95 light tank, was singled out in Japanese records for praise and credited with 18 hits against the American tanks with his 37mm gun. One Type 97 tank with the older 57mm gun was credited with knocking out five

M4A3 tanks. The attack petered out after about an hour of fighting. In total, one M4A3 was destroyed and four were disabled by Japanese fire; one was stuck in the irrigation ditch. In combination with previous casualties, these losses reduced the strength of Company C, 716th Tank Battalion, to a little more than half until the damaged tanks could be recovered.

Col Dalton in his later report complained that tanks were not very useful in attacks such as these across open ground. In retrospect, the tanks were used imprudently in view of the experiences several days earlier, when two M5A1 light tanks had been lost to heavy antitank fire. The 161st Infantry was not experienced in the use of tanks, and like many veteran units they tended to disparage Japanese antitank firepower. There was an unstated expectation that M4A3 medium tanks were essentially invulnerable to Japanese antitank guns, which was certainly the case with the old 37mm gun, but not with the new 47mm gun. The tanks could have remained at stand-off range providing fire support while the infantry secured the edge of the town. Once the initial antitank positions along the perimeter were cleared, the tanks could have joined the infantry at the town's

The 7th Tank Regiment deployed about half of its tanks in shallow revetments throughout San Manuel. This Type 97-kai had left the protection of its revetment, which is seen in the foreground. (NARA)

edge to begin the systematic block-by-block reduction. It's worth noting that this was the tactic used with the M7 105mm HMC self-propelled howitzers. These vehicles were organic to the regiment and Dalton recognized their vulnerability, and so kept them behind the infantry until the worst of the antitank defenses had been overcome.

The main attack against the north of the town started at 0725hrs by two companies of 2/161st Infantry, with the third company holding reserve positions on the ridge overlooking the town. The company on the right was forced to ground due to intense small-arms fire, while the company on the left penetrated about 50 yards into the northeast corner of the town before being stopped by machine-gun fire. They were then pushed out of the town by a Japanese counterattack supported by three tanks.

A second attempt to push into the town took place in the afternoon. The attack on the southwest corner of the town was renewed at 1400hrs, but was unable to push into this heavily defended sector. Around dusk, the company took up defensive positions behind the rice paddy dikes about 200 yards west of the town. Damaged tanks were recovered and made operable for the next day's fighting. American casualties for the day in this sector were eight killed and 63 wounded.

During the late morning and early afternoon, a tank-dozer was used to create a crude road from the northern ridge towards the northern side of the town, to allow heavier support to be brought up. The reinforcements consisted of two platoons from

The unit assigned to the reduction of San Manuel, the 161st Infantry, was made up of experienced Pacific veterans. These are the "Dirty Dozen," the surviving 13 officers from the original cadre of 114 officers who entered combat on Guadalcanal in 1942. They are seen in front of one of the captured Type 97-kai tanks in San Manuel on February 8, 1945, after the capture of the town. (NARA)

the regimental cannon company, each with two M7 105mm HMCs, and two platoons from the regimental antitank company with three 37mm antitank guns each. Around 1700hrs, after a five-minute artillery preparation, the two companies of 2/161st Infantry attacked into the town and secured a foothold. Facing them were five Type 97-kai tanks, three of which were in revetments, supported by Japanese infantry. The American infantry was brought under intense machine-gun and cannon fire from the tanks, but this time the Japanese tanks were engaged and knocked out by 37mm guns and 105mm howitzers. The American infantry secured a small number of buildings before setting up a defensive perimeter. After dark, the 7th Tank Regiment's maintenance section sent out a "suicide penetration team" against the 2/161st positions, and one of the M7 105mm HMCs was knocked out with a lunge-mine thrust against its side.

On January 25, 2/161st Infantry began a systematic block-by-block assault through the northern section of San Manuel. By this time, Company C, 716th Tank Battalion, had already moved into the northern part of the town to support the attack. The tactic was to assign an infantry scout to each tank or self-propelled howitzer. The scout would escort the vehicle commander forward and show him the intended target. The vehicle commander would then direct his tank or self-propelled howitzer forward to an advantageous position and destroy the emplaced Japanese tank or gun revetment. The M7 105mm HMC was generally preferred for this task, in spite of the open crew compartment. The much more powerful HE round of the 105mm howitzer was able to strip away camouflage on the Japanese revetments, and was more than adequate to demolish the lightly armored Japanese tanks. The attack pushed into the town far enough that on January 26, Company B, 2/161st Infantry, was sent around the eastern

Jap Tank Revetment Built Behind Rice Paddy Dike – A

side of the town to secure the bridge and road that constituted the main escape route out of the town towards St Nicolas. Since 1/161st Infantry had been frustrated by the heavy defenses in the southwestern corner of town, the battalion was ordered to pull back and join 2/161st Infantry in the push from the northern part of town. By January 27, most of the northern half of the town had been captured, and so a two-battalion attack with tank and M7 105mm HMC support began after another heavy artillery preparation. The regimental records recorded: "Though several (Japanese) tanks were eliminated, no more than 100 yards was gained along the front. Casualties were heavy. Fatigue is becoming apparent in attacking units."

With the defenses weakening, Shigemi ordered a final counterattack that night, starting shortly after midnight. The US regimental report described the attack:

About 0100 28 January the Japs, after a great deal of preliminary maneuvering, launched an attack with thirteen tanks. The point was well selected: a salient made by the left company of the right flank battalion (1/161st Infantry). Normal barrages of artillery and mortar were called in but did not quiet the Japs. The tanks assaulted in waves of three, each tank followed closely by foot troops. The tank assault position was about 100–150 yards from our foremost elements. Riflemen in pits opposed them with rifle AT grenades, bazookas and caliber .50 machine guns. Two 37mm guns had the tanks within range. The first tank was hit but overran the forward position, spraying blindly with machine guns and firing 47mm point-blank. Two AT guns set about 30

The 161st Infantry After-Action Report on the fighting at San Manuel was illustrated by this sketch by one of the unit's soldiers. It shows a Type 97-kai in its revetment, which had been carved into one of the dikes alongside the rice paddy at the edge of town. (NARA)

A destroyed Type 97-kai Shinhoto Chi-Ha, from a veteran's photo. The thin armor of this tank was badly overmatched by opposing weapons, and HE ammunition from either the 75mm tank gun or 105mm howitzer could blow open the tank, as is the case here. (Tom Laemlein)

to 40 yards in the rear of the front elements fired on the waves in turn. Ten of the tanks were halted, the leading one just 50 yards inside our front. All had been hit several times. Hits and penetrations were made with AT shells, AT grenades, bazookas and caliber .50 machine guns. Three tanks left the assault position and withdrew eastward out of town without attacking.

In the wake of the failed attack, Maj Gen Shigemi committed *hara-kiri* (ritual suicide) and surviving Japanese troops numbering about 400 men and seven tanks

More evidence of the vulnerability of the Type 97-kai can be seen in this veteran's shot. A 75mm or 105mm projectile has struck the left corner of the hull, peeling it open with catastrophic results for the crew inside. (Tom Laemlein)

fled out the southeastern side of town towards St Nicolas, which was held by the 10th Reconnaissance Regiment; about 200 of these troops were walking wounded. At 0930hrs, the two battalions of the 161st Infantry resumed the advance into the southern section of town against little opposition and the town was declared secure at 1330hrs on January 29 after six days of fighting.

Japanese casualties in the battle were about 755 killed; a handful of wounded soldiers were later found in the countryside, most often by Filipino guerilla forces. A total of 41 Type 97 medium tanks and four Type 95 light tanks were destroyed, as were all the Japanese artillery pieces.

IDA GROUP AT MUÑOZ

Following the reduction of San Manuel, the I Corps commander, Lt Gen Innis Swift, ordered the 6th and 25th Divisions to conduct a pincer movement against the main Japanese stronghold at San Jose. This maneuver led to two simultaneous tank battles with the Japanese 2nd Armored Division in the first week of February, with elements of the 25th Division attacking the Harada Group at Lupao and the 6th Division laying siege to the Ida Group in Muñoz.

The Ida Group in Muñoz was comparable in size to the Shigemi Group, with a strength of 48 Type 97 medium tanks, four Type 95 light tanks, four armored cars, and 1,800 troops; the group had a far more formidable antitank arsenal with 16 47mm antitank guns, as well as a battery of four 105mm field guns. As in the case of

The 20th Infantry at Muñoz were supported by a company of the 44th Tank Battalion. Some local Filipinos look over an M4 medium tank of Company A, 44th Tank Battalion, shortly after landing on White Beach in Lingayen Gulf at the start of the campaign in January 1945. The tank carries extensive markings, including a vehicle name starting with "Adulteress," while the nameplate in front of the commander's cupola is "Pat's Palace." (NARA)

the Shigemi Group, the Ida Group constructed a large number of tank revetments along the edge of the town, amplified with additional entrenchments inside the town itself.

The task of overcoming the Ida Group was assigned to the 20th RCT, which was based on the 20th Infantry, 6th Infantry Division, supported by Company C, 44th Tank Battalion and a company of the 98th Chemical Mortar Battalion. C/20th RCT began scouting the perimeter of Muñoz on the morning of January 28, 1945, and reported back that the town was held by a tank battalion. The town was heavily bombarded by both artillery and air strikes and hardly any buildings were still intact by the end of the month. On January 30, Col Washington Ives, the regimental commander, ordered two companies to conduct a reconnaissance in force of the village of Baloc on the road to Muñoz, as well as of Muñoz itself. B/20th RCT encountered heavy resistance at Baloc and took up defensive positions, while K/20th RCT set up defensive positions 600 yards from the town and sent out patrols.

On January 31, Baloc was assaulted by two companies from 1/20th RCT starting at 0800hrs, and the village was secured by mid afternoon. At the same time, K/20th RCT attacked into the northeast side of Muñoz, but was unable to secure more than a toe-hold in the town. Later in the day, the remainder of the 3rd Battalion, along with

Ida Group (Col Kumpai Ida, CO, 6th Tank Regiment)
3rd, 4th, 5th Companies, 6th Tank Regiment
8th Battery, 2nd Mobile Artillery Regiment
One company, 356th Infantry Battalion, 106th Division

The Ida Detachment attempted to withdraw out of Munoz north along Highway 5 on the night of February 6–7, 1945, but were caught by American roadblocks. This is a scene of the tail end of the column that was shot up by Company C, 44th Tank Battalion; one of the company's M4 tanks is evident in the background on the far left. The tank in the foreground is one of the older Type 97 Chi-Ha with 57mm gun, while the other two tanks evident to the left are both Type 97-kai Shinhoto Chi-Ha. (Tom Laemlein)

the attached 4.2in mortar company, was sent to Muñoz with the aim of securing the town the following day with a battalion-sized attack. On February 1, therefore, after a 15-minute artillery preparation by a single field artillery battalion, both companies attacked the town from the southwest. After the 3rd Battalion was halted by heavy Japanese fire, the 1st Battalion was added to the attack on their right flank. In view of the importance of securing Muñoz, I Corps sent three of its artillery battalions to provide fire-support to the 6th Division.

OVERLEAF

Gen. Isao Shigemi ordered the deployment of the 7th Tank Regiment's tanks in revetments around San Manuel. The revetments took advantage of the extensive vegetation around the town, including thick stands of bamboo. In addition, the town's periphery had a number of earth berms associated with dikes and other elements of the irrigation system for the paddies on the outskirts of town. As a result, the Type 97-kai Shinhoto Chi-Ha medium tanks and Type 95 Ha-Go light tanks were extremely well camouflaged on the morning of January 24 when the American attack began. The M4A3 tanks of Company C, 716th Tank Battalion began to advance towards the outskirts of town with the infantry of the 1st Battalion, 161st Infantry Regiment some distance behind. The infantry was not in close support of tanks since the artillery preparation continued until the tanks were only 300 yards from the town. The Japanese tankers exercised strict fire discipline and withheld fire until the American tanks had reached to only about 150 yards from their positions. The camouflage on the Japanese positions was so thorough that they could not be seen by the American tankers. The Japanese tankers were well aware that their tank guns were ineffective against the thick frontal armor of the American tanks, but they could penetrate their weaker side armor. At 150 yards, the Shigemi Group began taking the American tanks under fire, hitting them with a sudden volley from several tanks, a 47mm antitank gun, and two 105mm howitzers. Several tanks were hit in the original volley and came to a halt. One M4A3 tank was destroyed and four more were damaged. The tank attack faltered when a drainage ditch was encountered. One M4A3 crew attempted to get over the ditch by backing up, revving the engine, and jumping the ditch at full speed, but this only managed to get the tank bogged down on the far side of the ditch. The US tanks withdrew and took up overwatch positions to provide fire support for the 161st Infantry who began their attack on the town.

The fighting on February 2 gained no new ground for the 20th RCT, although an attempted counterattack by the Ida Group was repulsed with heavy Japanese casualties. The commander of the 6th Division, Maj Gen Edwin Patrick, became impatient with the progress of the attack and relieved Col Ives, replacing him with Lt Col Harold Maison. Patrick later regretted the decision when he realized that the size of the Ida Group had been substantially underestimated. The renewed attacks on February 3 included all three battalions of the 20th RCT along with tank support, but the fighting turned into a stubborn and frustrating block-by-block siege.

HARADA GROUP AT LUPAO

While the 20th RCT was entangled with the Ida Group at Muñoz, the 25th Division on its left was attempting to clear out the scattered 2nd Armored Division garrisons on the approaches to the main objective at Lupao. The Omura Detachment had been stationed at Gonzales during the third week of January, consisting of two batteries of Maj Kinjo Omura's 2nd Battalion, 2nd Motorized Artillery Regiment, and Capt Shoji Arao's 2nd Company, 6th Tank Regiment.

At 1800hrs on the night of January 29, the division ordered the detachment to retire from Gonzales and to move north of San Jose via the Pemienta–Umingan section of Highway 8. About two hours later, the column stumbled into the defensive perimeter of the 27th Infantry, 25th Division around Pemienta, which was supported by Company C, 716th Tank Battalion. A six-hour firefight ensued that lasted until dawn on January 30. In the process, the Omura Detachment was largely destroyed, its losses including eight Type 97-kai tanks, eight artillery tractors along with their 105mm howitzers, five trucks, and about 125 troops. The 27th Infantry faced far stiffer resistance up the road at Umingan, held by a battalion of the 26th Independent Mixed Regiment armed with at least eight 47mm antitank guns. When it failed to secure Umingan on February 1, the 25th Division ordered the neighboring 35th Infantry to bypass the town and proceed down Highway 8 towards Lupao. Highway 8 was the other main route to the San Jose junction, so was defended by the Harada Group in two clusters, first in Lupao and then in San Isidro further to the southeast.

The 35th Infantry reached the outskirts of Lupao on the afternoon of February 2, and the lead company was forced to ground by an intense barrage of tank and gun fire from the town defenses about 750 yards from the outskirts. Attempts to push into the town on February 3 were no more successful.

By now, the commanders of both the 6th and 25th Divisions recognized that Lupao and Muñoz were as heavily fortified as San Manuel. Unwilling to take heavy casualties to reduce these bastions, both divisions decided to continue the sieges to keep the Japanese forces in place, while other regiments bypassed them to secure the main objective at San Jose. As a result, on the afternoon of February 3, 3/35th Infantry swung around the main defenses of Lupao and set up a defensive barrier behind the town on Highway 8, to isolate Harada Group elements in Lupao from the garrison

down the road in San Isidro. At the same time, the 25th Division's other two regiments, the 27th and 161st Infantry, bypassed the fortified towns and headed cross-country for San Jose. Likewise, the 6th Division left the 20th RCT to reduce the Muñoz defenses, while the division's other regiments bypassed the city on either side. While both divisions were expecting a major fight for San Jose on February 4, it turned out to be an anticlimax. The 1st Infantry, 6th Division, marched into the city virtually unopposed on the morning of February 4 against a tiny Japanese rearguard, and secured the city by 1330hrs with very light casualties.

Both the US I Corps and the Japanese 2nd Armored Division were unaware that Gen Yamashita's 14th Area Army headquarters had issued instructions on February 4 for all units to withdraw. The main mission of the 2nd Armored Division had already been accomplished. The Japanese 105th Division had moved into the mountains on

On the night of January 29–30, 1945, the Omura Detachment attempted to withdraw from Gonzales to San Jose along the Pemienta–Umingan section of Highway 8. The column stumbled into American roadblocks including tanks of Company C, 716th Tank Battalion and was wiped out. This is one of eight Type 97-kai Shinhoto Chi-Ha's of Capt Shoji Arao's 2nd Company, 6th Tank Regiment, destroyed in the fighting. Spare tracks were attached to the turret front for additional protection, to no avail. (NARA)

Harada Group (Lt Col Kazuo Harada, CO, 10th Tank Regiment)
2nd Company, 7th Tank Regiment
2nd, 3rd, 4th Companies, 10th Tank Regiment
3rd Antitank Gun Company

The Omura Detachment was based around Maj Kinjo Omura's 2nd Battalion, 2nd Motorized Artillery Regiment, and it was destroyed in the fighting on the night of January 29–30 on Highway 8. Here is an Isuzu Type 98 Shi-Ke 4-ton prime mover and its associated 105mm Type 91 howitzer. (NARA)

February 2 and the supply dumps in and around San Jose had been safely transferred. Gen Iwanaka's 2nd Armored Division headquarters did not receive the withdrawal order until February 6.

By this time, the Ida Group in Muñoz had been battered by several days of fighting and had lost 35 tanks. There were five US artillery battalions bombarding the town and Col Ida had been killed by artillery fire. The garrison was ignorant about the configuration of US forces in its area and decided to attempt a breakout on the night of February 6–7, not realizing that the escape route was firmly in American hands. Around 0300hrs, a diversionary attack by four tanks supported by infantry was launched against the 35th Infantry, while the main column headed out of town on Highway 5 towards San Jose.

The US 6th Division had numerous forces in the vicinity of the highway, and began to rake the column with fire. The column first ran into roadblocks established by the 63rd Infantry, but then were brought under point-blank fire by 105mm and 155mm howitzers of the 53rd and 80th Field Artillery Battalions. An M4 tank company of the 44th Tank Battalion destroyed much of the tail of the column not already blasted by the artillery and small-arms fire. Unable to see the column in the dark, the M4 tank gunners improvised by spraying the area with co-axial .30cal machine-gun fire, and when a tracer ricocheted off the armor, the 75mm gun was fired. After a few vehicles were hit, the fires began to illuminate the column. A few hundred Japanese troops were able to escape the carnage under the cover of darkness, but all of the surviving tanks and heavy equipment in the column were destroyed. Japanese casualties in the escape attempt were 247 troops, ten Type 97 medium tanks, one Type 95 light tank, ten trucks, and two artillery tractors with their 105mm howitzers. Total Japanese casualties during the battle of Muñoz were 52 tanks and 1,527 troops. US casualties were 47 killed, 164 wounded, and one M7 105mm HMC destroyed.

The Harada Group in Lupao and San Isidro took another course of action and planned to sabotage most surviving vehicles and heavy equipment, and slip away into the mountains at night. In Lupao, one tank detachment of 10–11 tanks attempted to race out of the town in the darkness. About half were destroyed by the 35th Infantry cordon, while five escaped into the hills. Lupao was cleared on February 8 and the casualty list for the Harada Group was 900 troops, 33 tanks, 26 trucks, and three 75mm field guns. The 35th Infantry had suffered 95 men killed and 270 wounded in the fighting for Lupao. The elements of the Harada Group in San Isidro had not

The two Type 1 Ho-Ni gun tanks of the 2nd Mobile Artillery Regiment were deployed in camouflaged revetments near Aritao and Sante Fe. This one was captured by the 37th Division near Santa Fe on June 2, 1945. (NARA)

been directly attacked and had received instructions to withdraw earlier than in the other towns. As a result, the detachment abandoned the town on the night of February 5–6. When the town was occupied by the 161st Infantry on February 6, there were 23 tanks, 18 trucks, and two 75mm field guns abandoned or destroyed in the town.

By the end of the first week of February, the Japanese 2nd Armored Division in the northern Luzon sector had lost about 180 tanks as well as most of its artillery equipment, and about 2,000 troops. By the first week of March after the northern Luzon area had been scoured, the tally rose to 197 Chi-Ha and 19 Ha-Go tanks from the 230 Chi-Ha and 35 Ha-Go tanks eventually found on Luzon at the end of

One of the more unusual vehicles operated by the Engineer Regiment of the Japanese 2nd Armored Division was the Type 96 SS Armored Engineer Vehicle. They were multi-purpose vehicles based on the Type 89 medium tank and could be used for obstacle-clearing, bridge-laying, and flame-throwing. They were built primarily for attacking Soviet fortified positions along the Manchurian border. The vehicle here is an SS Model Bo, from the fifth and final production batch. Flamethrowers can be seen in both the front and side positions. Eight of these were captured on Luzon of two different versions, mostly during the fighting near Aritao in June 1945. (NARA)

hostilities. Additional elements of the division with the Kembu Group around Clark Field were destroyed there during the fighting in late January 1945. Lt Matsumoto's 8th Independent Tank Company, part of the Yanagimoto Detachment, was decimated in a counterattack on the afternoon of January 29.

Although the Japanese 2nd Armored Division had lost nearly all of its tanks, tank crews, motorized infantry units, and other heavy equipment, it continued to fight through the end of the Philippines campaign. Yamashita's 14th Area Army used the headquarters and service element to reconstitute it as an improvised infantry division. The division's only intact tank unit was the 5th Tank Company, 10th Tank Regiment, which had been sent into the mountains near Baguio prior to the January–February fighting. Curiously enough, this unit took part in one of the last tank-vs-tank actions of the Philippines fighting in mid April 1945, when Yamashita ordered surviving tanks converted into *kamikaze* weapons.

A Type 97 medium tank and a Type 95 light tank had explosives fitted to the hull front and they were assigned to the defenses in the Irisan gorge area, which was being attacked by the US 148th Infantry. The tanks waited in ambush in a bamboo stand on the road between Baguio and Sablan, and when US M4 medium tanks of the 3rd Platoon, Company B, 775th Tank Battalion, appeared around the bend in Route 9 on the morning of April 17, the first American tank was hit and disabled by 47mm gunfire. The tank behind attempted to back up out of trouble, but instead it fell off the road and plunged into the gorge 400ft below. While medics attempted to recover the wounded under the cover of the third tank, the two Japanese tanks raced forward and rammed the damaged tank as well as the third tank in the column, but the explosives failed to detonate. The gunner had remained in the first, damaged Sherman and fired at the attacking Japanese tank at point-blank range, knocking it out. The other Japanese tank was hit by fire from Shermans further back in the column.

STATISTICS AND ANALYSIS

Although the 2nd Armored Division accomplished its last-minute assignment of shielding San Jose, the cost of this mission was exorbitant, and Yamashita had to sacrifice his original intention of using the division on the Central Plains to delay the American advance on Clark Field and Manila. The decision to expend the division's tank regiments as a disconnected string of fortified towns was criticized as wasteful if not inept by other Japanese commanders.

The fate of the Japanese 2nd Armored Division in northern Luzon was influenced by the shortcomings of the IJA's armor doctrine and technological priorities. The configuration of the division was not well suited to a defensive role in the Philippines due to its weak infantry component. Yamashita was indifferent to the use of the division as a unified force, and immediately began breaking it up into small battlegroups. These might have been better suited to local conditions than an intact division had they been balanced combined-arms teams. However, the decision to strip away two of the three infantry battalions from the division for the defense of Clark Field only exacerbated the division's chronic weakness in infantry and degraded the combat capability of the three main battlegroups in northern Luzon. The deficiencies might have been remedied by attaching infantry from neighboring infantry divisions, as was done in one case with the Ida Group at Muñoz, which substantially improved its defensive capabilities. The severe shortage of infantry left the three main battlegroups in northern Luzon almost entirely isolated and blind, and the attacking US infantry divisions were able to bypass them at will, as was most evident in the eventual seizure of San Jose.

The tactical choices available to Japanese commanders on Luzon were to some extent dictated by the technological shortcomings of Japanese armor at this stage of the war. The neglect of tank development and production after the late 1930s left the IJA with a tank force dependent on obsolete tanks and inadequate antitank weapons. The Type 97-kai Shinhoto Chi-Ha could not compete against the M4A3 Sherman tank and it was vulnerable to the whole gamut of American antitank weapons, even marginal weapons such as rifle grenades that were nearly useless in the 1944–45 fighting in Europe.

The US Army's M4A3 medium tank was more than adequate in tank-vs-tank fighting with the Type 97-kai, but in reality such actions were only a minor aspect of the M4's combat use in the Pacific. For the vast majority of missions, the M4A3 was used to support infantry against Japanese defensive emplacements. It was adequate in this role, but far from ideal. The Sherman tank family had been developed for use by both armored divisions and the separate tank battalions; it was better suited to the armored divisions than to the separate tank battalions with a greater emphasis on mobility and reliability than on armor and firepower. In the infantry support role, the M4A3 needed

Based on the Philippines experience, the practice of embedding tanks as fixed fortifications became common in the later campaigns of 1945. This Type 97-kai Shinhoto Chi-Ha of the 26th Tank Regiment on Iwo Jima was dug in on Hill 382, which provided an excellent field of fire against Airfield No. 2 seen beyond. The vehicle here is a command tank, evident from the radio mast fitting on the right rear fender. (NARA)

weapons better suited to fire support, such as more 105mm assault guns and flamethrower tanks. The US Army was very slow in deploying flamethrower tanks to the Pacific. A small flamethrower tank detachment was deployed on Luzon in the final phase of the campaign and the first widespread Army flamethrower use did not come until the Okinawa campaign in the summer of 1945 with the 713th Tank Battalion (Flamethrower).

The main drawback of US Army tanks in the Pacific fighting was not technological but tactical – the long-standing neglect of tank–infantry tactics until well into 1943.[5] The decision by Headquarters AGF to keep the tank battalion as a separate unit, not organic to the infantry divisions, was unfortunate, since it did not foster the type of common training and mutual understanding that was possible. In many cases, this organizational shortcoming could be avoided by joint training. Indeed, the 716th Tank Battalion had been deployed with the 43rd Division prior to Operation *Mike-1* on Luzon, and conducted joint training of tank companies and infantry regiments. This cooperation was instrumental in the solid performance of the tank companies

5. For a more detailed description of the problems with US Army tank–infantry support doctrine, see Steven J. Zaloga, *US Tank and Tank Destroyer Battalions in the ETO 1944–45*, Battle Orders 10, Osprey, Oxford (2005)

that fought alongside the 43rd Division at various points in the Luzon campaign, as displayed by Company B, 716th Tank Battalion, in the fighting in the Cabaruan Hills prior to the San Manuel action. However, Company C, 716th Tank Battalion, was split off from the division to support the 161st Infantry for the reduction of San Manuel, and neither unit had any prior training together. The 161st Infantry was never entirely comfortable with the attached tank company, and preferred to use its organic cannon company with M7 105mm HMC self-propelled howitzers, in spite of their vulnerability in the close-combat role. These problems could have been alleviated by a common US Army training program for tank–infantry tactics, but such a program did not exist in 1944.

The related technological dimension of this problem was the inadequate attention shown to tank–infantry communication. In 1944, US Army tank radios could not communicate with US infantry platoon and company radios. Various fixes were improvised in the field, such as mounting field telephones onto armor and jury-rigging the infantry SCR-300 radio inside the tanks. These approaches were already under way in the European theater in the autumn of 1944 and in US Marine Corps tank battalions in the summer of that year, but US Army tank battalions had such limited and scattered combat use until the Philippines campaign that the need for such communication improvements was late. An Army after-action report on the use of tanks on Leyte provides a concise survey of the issues:

> A direct result of the lack of [common] training was a feeling of distrust between the two arms. It evolved from the misunderstanding of each others' capabilities and limitations. Infantry commanders felt that the tanks were not sufficiently aggressive when they wouldn't push blindly out in face of an enemy who had stopped the foot soldiers. In return, the tanker felt that when the going got stiff and the lead started flying the infantryman would desert him. If the tank couldn't see the accompanying infantry, he immediately surmised that he had been abandoned, not realizing that in the close underbrush, the infantryman was still there, but had merely crouched down to avoid being a larger target. The situation was further aggravated by the lack of tank–infantry communications, and the whole business became a major problem when the weather, heat, and mud increased. It finally straightened itself out as the tankers and infantrymen became used to working with each other and learned, expensively to be sure, just what each could, would, and was prepared to do in support of each other. By the end of the campaign, the tank–infantry team was pretty well coordinated and bound together by mutual trust and respect.

What the report did not mention was that following the end of the Leyte campaign in December 1944, the same set of problems cropped up in January 1945 when tank battalions were used in support of infantry on Luzon. There was no organizational or training system in place to transmit these "lessons learned" within the Army's SWPA command.

In general, the US Army in the Pacific was much slower in adapting the tank to Pacific conditions than the US Marine Corps, since the Marines began using medium

tanks in the Central Pacific nearly a year earlier. The Marine tank battalions were already addressing Japanese antitank tactics by early 1944 through the use of appliqué armor, and began dealing with the 47mm gun threat with a thickened version of the appliqué armor in Peleliu in September 1944. They also began fielding flamethrower tanks to deal with Japanese fortifications more than a year before the Army. The Marine Corps showed a more developed awareness of tank–infantry coordination and was addressing the tank–infantry communication problem at the time of the Marshalls campaign in February 1944. Since the Marine tank battalions wcre organic to their divisions by 1943, joint training came sooner in the war and became more routine. In spite of these problems, the adaptability of the Army separate tank battalions made them an essential tool in offensive operations in the Pacific wherever the terrain permitted.

The US Army was slow to adopt flame tanks to deal with Japanese fortified positions. The Flame Tank Detachment, with four of these M5A1 light tanks converted with the E7-7 (Q Model) Flame Thrower, was deployed in April 1945 to support the 25th Division in the mountain fighting in northern Luzon. The fighting re-affirmed the shortcomings of light tanks in the flame tank role, a conclusion that had been reached a year earlier by the Marine tank battalions. (NARA)

BIBLIOGRAPHY

The destruction of the Japanese 2nd Armored Division on Luzon has been treated as part of the Philippines campaign in general histories, but there has been no detailed account in English. This book was based primarily on archival records. The US side of the battle of San Manuel and the other Luzon tank battles comes mainly from unit after-action reports, including those of the 716th Tank Battalion, the 161st Infantry, and several other tank battalions and infantry regiments.

Since the Japanese government ordered the destruction of military records in the period from the surrender to US occupation, the best remaining sources are US intelligence records and the reconstructed Japanese accounts that were undertaken by the Demobilization Bureau after the war in occupied Japan, and known as the "Japanese Monograph" series. The most detailed accounts are in the various G-2 (intelligence) sections at various command levels, and I examined the G-2 records of the 6th and 25th Divisions, I Corps, and the 6th Army at the National Archives and Records Administration (NARA) in College Park, MD. These contain a large amount of detail about the order of battle of the 2nd Armored Division, plus equipment holdings and losses, captured Japanese unit records, translated diaries of Japanese soldiers, and interrogation reports of troops of the 2nd Armored Division. The G-2 records of the 25th Division are especially detailed on the 2nd Armored Division, while the higher commands offer more comprehensive analytic surveys. The details of Japanese tank production come from the unpublished records and reports of the US Strategic Bombing Survey, also located at NARA.

GOVERNMENT REPORTS

Enemy on Luzon: An Intelligence Summary, US Sixth Army (1945)
Japanese Employment of Tanks on Luzon, Far East Report No. 165, US Army Forces
    (1945)

Philippine Operation Record – Phase III: January–August 1945, Japanese Monograph No. 7

Reports of General MacArthur: Japanese Operations in the Southwest Pacific Area Volume II – Part I, Japanese Demobilization Bureaux (1966)

Balthis, Maj J. L. et al., *Armor on Okinawa: The Tank Infantry Team*, Armor School (1949)

Garay, Maj Stephen, *The Breach of Intramuros (Manila)*, Armor School (1948)

Hunt, Maj Milton, *Use of Armor in Luzon*, Armor School (1948)

Kane, Capt Michael, *The Operations of the 20th Infantry (6th Inf. Div.) at Munoz, Luzon 30 Jan to 8 Feb 1945: Annihilation of a Japanese Tank Regiment by a US Infantry Regiment*, Infantry School (1947)

Seneff, Lt Col George et al., *Armor on Leyte, Sixth Army Operations 17 Oct–26 Dec 44*, Armor School (1949)

ARTICLES

Bogart, Charles, "Japanese Second Tank Division on Luzon," *AFV News*, Part 1 (May 1982) pp.2–5; Part 2 (September 1982) pp.2–3

Holzimmer, Kevin, "In Close Country: World War II American Armor Tactics in the Jungles of the Southwest Pacific," *Armor* (July–August 1997) pp.21–31

Zaloga, Steven, "Japanese Armor on Corregidor," *AFV News* (September 1982) pp.18–19

BOOKS

Dick, Robert, *Cutthroats: The Adventures of a Sherman Tank Driver in the Pacific*, Presidio, New York (2006)

Drea, Edward, *Japan's Imperial Army: Its Rise and Fall, 1853–1945*, University Press of Kansas, Lawrence, KS (2009)

McLean, Donald (ed.), *Japanese Tanks, Tactics, & Anti-Tank Weapons*, Normount, Wickenburg, AR (1973)

Rottman, Gordon, and Akira Takizawa, *World War II Japanese Tank Tactics*, Osprey, Oxford (2008)

Salecker, Gene, *Rolling Thunder against the Rising Sun: The Combat History of US Army Tank Battalions in the Pacific in World War II*, Stackpole, Mechanicsburg, PA (2008)

Smith, Robert, *Triumph in the Philippines*, US Army Chief of Military History (1963)

Zaloga, Steven J., *Armour of the Pacific War*, New Vanguard 35, Osprey, Oxford (1983)

Zaloga, Steven J., *Japanese Tanks 1939–45*, New Vanguard 137, Osprey, Oxford (2007)

Zaloga, Steven J., *Tank Battles of the Pacific War*, Concord, Hong Kong (1995)

INDEX